*What Christians Really Believe—
and Why*

Other books by
STANLEY J. GRENZ
published by Westminster John Knox Press

Sexual Ethics: An Evangelical Perspective

The Social God and the Relational Self:
A Trinitarian Theology of the Imago Dei

Welcoming but Not Affirming:
An Evangelical Response to Homosexuality

WITH JOHN R. FRANKE

Beyond Foundationalism:
Shaping Theology in a Postmodern Context

What Christians Really Believe— and Why

STANLEY J. GRENZ

Westminster John Knox Press

LOUISVILLE • LONDON

Unless otherwise indicated, scripture quotations are from the
New Revised Standard Version of the Bible, Copyright © 1989 by the
Division of Christian Education of the National Council of Churches
of Christ in the U.S.A., and are used by permission.

Scripture quotations marked NIV are from
The Holy Bible, New International Version.
Copyright © 1973, 1978, 1984 International Bible Society.
Used by permission of Zondervan Bible Publishers.

Book design by Jennifer K. Cox
Cover design by Pam Poll

First Edition
Published by Westminster John Knox Press
Louisville, Kentucky

This book is printed on acid-free paper that meets the
American National Standards Institute Z39.48 standard. ∞

PRINTED IN THE UNITED STATES OF AMERICA
04 05 06 07 — 10 9 8 7 6

Library of Congress Cataloging-in-Publication Data

Grenz, Stanley, date.
    What Christians really believe—and why / Stanley J. Grenz. — 1st ed.
      p. cm.
    Includes bibliographical references.
    ISBN 0-664-25732-1 (alk. paper)
    1. Theology, Doctrinal.   2. Evangelicalism—Doctrines.   I. Title.
BT75.2.G745   1998
230—dc21   97-44956

To Lyle W. Grenz, D.C.

in gratitude for his encouragement and support

Contents

Introduction

Relationships . . .
Economic well-being . . .
Family . . .
Health . . .

*E*ach of us is concerned about matters such as these. Our thoughts, our worries, our plans so often focus on these things. These concerns can consume our waking moments and invade our sleep.

Yet often hidden just beneath the surface of our day-to-day lives is another, deeper concern that gives shape to and drives how we pursue these things. Lying at the depth of our being is an aching for inner peace and a craving for a sense of purpose.

In a manner unparalleled in recent times, people today are embarking on a personal quest, hoping to discover these elusive realities. The cover of a recent issue of Canada's leading newsmagazine, *Maclean's,* recently highlighted this. The headline declared, "Mainstream North America searches for meaning in life."[1]

But where can we turn for answers to the crucial questions we raise? Where can we find the sense of well-being for which we hunger?

Today we are being bombarded with a dazzling array of proposals about where the answers can be found. People today are confused by the chorus of discordant voices calling to us from every conceivable direction. Yet they find themselves driven by the consumer mentality indicative of contemporary society to return again and again to the smorgasbord of current options. Consequently, they move en masse from fad to fad, each one following the crowd in a desperate attempt to keep up with the latest "rage." Thus, North Americans gobble up the "how to" books, sign up for the latest therapy conference, or hop from church to church in hope of finding what they are looking for.

One recent fad is the ancient Chinese practice of *feng shui* (Chinese for "wind" and "water"). Hoping to catch the wave of popular interest, Nancy SantoPietro, a psychotherapist turned feng shui specialist, placed an advertisement in a New York newspaper. Need a job? Looking for a lover? The ad claimed that the principles of feng shui can help with matters such as these. Through the ancient principles of feng shui, the ad promised, "you can change your environment and change your life." How? To cite one example: SantoPietro counsels people who are plagued by interpersonal problems to "hang a pink shui crystal on a nine-inch red string in your relationship corner."[2]

In the end, however, today's seekers all too often find they are little more than spiritual voyeurs. The closest many ever come to laying hold of their dreams is to put themselves wistfully into the glowing stories of how their fellow travelers found the secret of life.

In a society in which beliefs are in constant flux, confusion abounds. People—including many Christians—are unsure about where they should turn. There is even much puzzlement about what the Christian faith actually teaches about these matters: What *do* Christians believe? What response does Christianity offer to the crucial, perennial questions of human existence? And how do these beliefs square with various proposals and theories propagated in our society?

My task is to clarify what Christians really do believe. The following chapters offer a summary of the fundamental beliefs of the Christian faith. Hence, this is a book of Christian doctrine or theology. Yet it doesn't follow the usual format. It doesn't progress through the major doctrines of the church in the typical order—God, humanity, Christ, the Spirit, the church, and last things. Instead, I place the Christian teaching about these topics within the context of the grave existential questions we all face.

What are these crucial questions? At one point or another, each of us must come to grips with seven central issues involving our existence. These queries follow a somewhat logical progression:

Why believe at all?
Who am I and why am I here?
Are we alone in the universe?
Which God?
Who is Jesus (and what did he do)?
What am I searching for and how do I find it?
Where is the universe . . . where am I . . . going?

This book presents aspects of Christian doctrine in the context of the queries we find lodged within the recesses of our being. My intent is to show how the answers to these questions can be found in the teachings of the church as derived from the Bible, the sourcebook of Christian belief.

NOTES

1. *Maclean's* 107, no. 41 (October 10, 1994).
2. Sharon Doyle Driedger, "Promise of Prosperity: Fad or Fact, Feng Shui Is All the Rage," *Maclean's* 110, no. 17 (April 28, 1997): 56–57.\

Chapter 1
Why Believe?

Who am I and why am I here? Are we alone in the universe? What is God like? What am I searching for? What happens when I die?

At one time or another we all ask questions such as these. In fact, one crucial task we each face is to determine personal answers to the deep, foundational questions we raise about life itself.

One intriguing characteristic of these queries is the form that our answers to them always take. The conclusions we eventually draw to the "big" existential questions of life come as statements about beliefs. We respond by declaring, "I believe . . ." In this manner, every attempt to give a credible response to the deepest questions of human existence leads us inevitably into the realm of faith.

Faith? At first, you may recoil at the very thought of speaking about faith. Perhaps you link being a person of faith with suddenly changing into a fanatic, a "true believer." Maybe you don't relish the thought of becoming like that person you once knew who was always spouting Bible verses or the two tract-peddlers who rang your doorbell last month.

Although many people today share your reticence, they are increasingly finding themselves searching for something to hold on to. They have set out on a quest to discover the meaning of life, and to find personal wholeness and inner peace.

Take Roger, the office manager in the comic strip "Betty," for example. One installment depicted Roger sauntering up to the leading character's desk. He asked his employee about the latest activities of one of her colleagues, Bea, who was known for her penchant for latching on to the latest fad. Roger wanted to know if Bea was indeed giving psychic readings in the employee lounge.

After confirming the rumor, Betty inquired about her boss's motives. She asked him point blank if he was a "true believer." Feeling a bit put off by this suggestion, the executive responded nonchalantly. He informed her that today's manager can't rule out anything that might give him an edge on the competition.

Like Roger, our skeptical side demands that we resist becoming true believers. Yet our pragmatic nature requires that we keep our options open: There just might be something to it all. More significantly, we discover within ourselves the gnawing question of belief.

This leads us back to the question of faith: How should we respond to a world that continually bombards us with new beliefs and truth claims? In a society like ours, how can anyone advocate holding fast to a particular set of beliefs? And in the end, does what *anyone* believes really make any difference? In this chapter we tackle these questions head on. Our goal is to search out a foundation for believing. To this end, we must raise the preliminary, foundational queries: What does it mean to believe? And are beliefs at all significant?

What Does It Mean to Believe?

The term *faith* (or *believing*) stands near the top of the list of today's most misunderstood concepts. What is faith? What does it mean to believe?

Mistaken Views of Faith

Throughout much of the twentieth century, the idea of having faith was suspect, and persons of faith were placed on the defensive. In part, this situation occurred because many people misunderstood what faith is about. Several erroneous conceptions have been widespread in our society.

Accepting the Incredible. One such misconception linked faith with accepting what is impossible and nonsensical. To believe, many people assumed, requires that a person commit intellectual suicide. In a scientifically oriented culture people thought that a truly learned person could accept only what can be proved through the scientific method. They warned against taking anything "by faith," that is, without its being substantiated scientifically. Only by a sheer "will to believe," they thought, can people of faith accept a host of what to these critics seemed to be at best pure nonsense and at worst irrational superstitions—whether they affirm the existence of demons and guardian angels or a God who is three-in-one.

Lewis Carroll's popular story *Through the Looking Glass* provides a lucid example of this popular, yet erroneous assumption. One day Alice (of *Alice in Wonderland* fame) was discussing the whole matter of faith with the White Queen.[1] The Queen began by offering Alice something to believe, namely, that the woman is very old—"a hundred and one, five months and a day" to be exact. Alice, of course, replied that she simply couldn't believe that. In response the Queen admonished the little girl in a pitying tone, "Try again; draw a long breath, and shut your eyes." Alice laughed. "There is no use trying," she said. "One can't believe impossible things."

At this point, the Queen, in her best condescending tone, offered her diagnosis of Alice's problem: "I dare say you haven't had much practice. When I was your age, I always did it for half an hour a day. Why sometimes I've believed as many as six impossible things before breakfast."

The realm beyond the looking glass—the domain of the White Queen—is a place where sheer belief, and hence nonsense, reigns. As this parody indicates, to the scientific mind, belief can only mean accepting what is irrational. And to describe faith in this manner is to dismiss it immediately.

While faith may at one time have been rejected as blind belief in the incredible, this view is no longer as widely held. Many people today do not equate faith with the blind acceptance of nonsensical, scientifically unprovable ideas. But with what understanding have they replaced it?

Leaping into the Unknown. Sad to say, some have rejected one erroneous conception for another. To them faith is a leap into a realm beyond the visible. Through faith, we grasp what we cannot perceive through the senses. And consequently faith involves the ability to remain steadfast in one's resolve even in the face of contrary evidence.

An episode of *Star Trek: The Next Generation* ("Rightful Heir") illustrates this understanding of faith. The Klingon member of the Enterprise crew, Lt. Worf, had embarked on a spiritual quest that took him into the ancient lore of his society. His odyssey was fueled by the appearance of someone who claimed to be the long-awaited Klingon messiah. The claimant, however, turned out to be a fraud. In the midst of the crisis of faith that followed this disappointing discovery, Worf turned to his android friend, Data, for solace.

Attempting to assist Worf through this difficult time, the wise starship officer mused about a somewhat similar crisis he went through when his creators told him he was just a machine. Despite such shattering news, Data reported, he simply chose to believe that he had the potential to be more than a collection of circuits and subprocessors. How had he come to this decision? Data's reply was simple: "I made a leap of faith."

There is a sense, of course, in which Data was correct. Faith is at times a leap beyond what can be substantiated by available evidence. Yet this characterization of faith lands a bit wide of the mark. It all-too-readily risks confusing "believing" with "making believe."

Perhaps as a child you lived out a fantasy about an imaginary friend with whom you could play and converse. Or perhaps you talked about imaginary creatures such as unicorns. This is the realm of "make-believe." But this is not where faith takes us.

To view "believing" as a leap is to fail to see the connection between faith commitment and the intellectual dimension of life. Faith is not the affirmation of what is in fact utter nonsense. It is not an unwarranted leap beyond appearance. Nor is it simply choosing to believe something, somewhat akin to "make-believe."

What then is faith?

Faith as Knowledge, Assent, and Trust

Properly understood, faith always remains grounded in the intellect, even though it never remains merely on the intellectual level. Rightly understood, faith affirms that in some sense what I believe is true regardless of my affirming its truth. Perhaps we can better understand this connection between belief and the intellectual dimension of life by viewing faith as a three-step progression that begins with knowledge, moves to assent, and reaches its goal in trust.[2]

Knowledge. Faith begins with knowledge. In this context, "knowing" simply means being informed about something. Someone tells you something. Through this, you come to know something about which you were previously ignorant. In this sense, faith begins with an assertion about reality that at least in theory is open for exploration and discussion. As assertions, these are fundamentally intellectual.

Assent. Knowledge, in turn, gives rise to assent. This is the intellectual act of acknowledging that the information you received is true. Assent involves agreeing with or accepting the claim about the nature of reality that has come your way. Such assent may be expressed verbally. Its verbal expression readily takes the form: "I believe that . . ."

To see this, look at the following statements:

"I believe that snow is white."

"I believe that by freeing the slaves, Abraham Lincoln served his country well."

"I believe that when I die the angels will carry my soul to heaven."

These three declarations differ greatly from each other. The first reflects a conclusion drawn from observation of a natural phenomenon. The second offers an opinion about the contribution of a historical figure. The third presents a conviction about matters that transcend earthly life. Despite these differences in content, however, the statements share the same structure: "I believe that . . ." Each is an acknowledgment that something is true. Each articulates intellectual assent to a claim about some aspect of reality.

Trust. Faith involves knowledge plus personal assent; that is, with faith one accepts certain statements as true. Hence, at its foundation, faith includes an intellectual component. But faith moves one step further. It culminates with trust. Trust occurs when the knower personally appropriates the known, acknowledged truth. It involves entrusting yourself to the truth about reality you have come to know and accept.

We engage this kind of faith continuously both in the large and the small aspects of life. Consider a mundane example. Needing to furnish your new apartment, you make your way to the local furniture store one Saturday morning. As you browse through the showroom, you spy an easy chair. The salesperson rushes over to you and extols the chair's virtues. It incorporates the latest design in easy chairs, she reports, and therefore people of every shape and size will find it comfortable.

Her presentation has led you to the first stage along the road to faith—knowledge.

"So what do you think?" the salesperson asks as you stand beside the chair deep in thought. After a lengthy pause you respond: "Yes, I think you're right. This new design is a great improvement. The chair should serve me well. And it's just what my living room needs."

You have come to the point of assent. You have accepted the knowledge you gained.

But then you continue to stand motionless in front of the chair. A puzzled look comes across the salesperson's face. "When is this customer going to get on with it?" she wonders. What action does the salesperson anticipate from you? She expects that knowledge and assent will evoke something else—trust. She wants you to entrust yourself or commit yourself; she is waiting for you to purchase the chair.

Only with this step is faith truly present, for knowledge and assent alone are not faith. Faith requires trust.

I took this example, of course, from a trivial aspect of life. We would not even think about the role of faith in such mundane matters. The knotty question of faith arises when we come to the important beliefs people espouse. What happens when we entertain convictions that focus on the "bigger" dimensions of existence, such as God, our human purpose, or life after death? What about beliefs that attempt to bring our entire world into some sort of unified whole? Dare we give intellectual assent to statements that operate in this deeper sphere? Is it possible to have firm convictions that are deeper, convictions we call "religious"? Is it truly possible to believe *anything* about such matters as God, the world as a whole, and my place in the cosmos?

Is It Possible
to Believe Anything?

As I noted earlier, many people in the twentieth century responded to this question with a resounding "No!" This type of belief is impossible. We cannot introduce faith into the equation, they argued. Why not? According to some people, we should accept only what can be proved scientifically. Answers that require faith to substantiate them, they said categorically, lack the kind of certainty that a scientific age and a scientific mind demand.

Not surprisingly, this posture readily led to a narrow perspective. Under the onslaught of the "scientific method," many people concluded that our sphere of existence must be limited to the physical dimension of life. And accepting this, they felt it necessary to eliminate the "spiritual" from consideration.

Faith and the Age of Spirituality

Times are changing, however. We are entering a new era, the age of spirituality.[3] In Canada, for example, not only do eight out of ten adults say they believe in God, 82 percent consider themselves to be "somewhat" or "very spiritual." And about half report that their lives have become more spiritual in the last several years.[4]

Does this mean that people today are religious? Not necessarily. Many people draw a clear distinction between "spirituality" and "religion," understood as personal involvement in religious practices. Hence, despite statistics indicating a widespread belief in God, less than 25 percent of adult Canadians attend church regularly. Both in Canada and the United States adherence to mainline Christian churches is continuing its downward plunge unabated, perhaps foreshadowing the death of organized religion as it has been traditionally understood.

Yet this decline does not necessarily signal that people are not interested in spirituality. David Batstone, who teaches religion at the University of San Francisco, reported that although 80 percent of his students claim that they are "not religious," the same number also think of themselves as "spiritual."[5] Findings such as these led one Roman Catholic bishop to conclude, "While the physical membership of churches is collapsing all around us . . . words like 'values,' 'soul' and 'spirit' are coming back into ordinary discourse. People are as spiritually inclined as ever, in the sense that they still dream, they still have visions and aspirations for a better world, they still look for some kind of paradise."[6]

What does all this have to say about faith and believing? Whether or not it translates into a revival of traditional religious practice, the dawn of an age of spirituality suggests that rather than being banished by the relentless advance of modern science, faith remains a perennial dimension of human existence. In the face of life—and death—humans desperately look for a source of strength. But finding strength requires faith. Consequently, a world beset with a sense of tragedy leads many people to conclude that faith is possible, even necessary.

Faith in a Pluralist Age?

Faith is indeed possible. Nevertheless, the mood of our time still advises that we look askance at people of steadfast conviction. Having firm convictions and standing firm in one's convictions is considered inappropriate. What exactly is it about our world that makes holding firm convictions repugnant? The answer is quite simple: pluralism.

We live in a pluralistic society. We are continually bombarded with competing assertions about what is ultimately true and with competing visions of reality. Around us is a discordant chorus of voices, each one claiming to tell us what we should believe—each one admonishing us to embrace the "truth" it proclaims. The myriad of competing claims that characterizes our world leads us almost inevitably to ask rhetorically, "With so many opinions vying for attention, how can anyone possibly be dogmatic about anything?" In such an environment, the preferred stance can only be openness, tolerance, even affirmation of all viewpoints. For after all, who knows who is right?

Where pluralism reigns, the worst crime you can commit is to believe anything firmly. Why are beliefs suspect in a pluralist context? One reason is that pluralism must defend itself. Pluralists fear that holding steadfastly to convictions inevitably leads to intolerance. And intolerance, of course, poses a threat to pluralism.

This fear came to expression in a bizarre incident that happened in Montreal in 1995. A man filed a petition in court claiming that the Bible contravenes the Canadian Charter of Rights and Freedoms. The book should be banned from public places, he asserted, because both Testaments "promote violence, racism, discrimination and incite incest."[7]

Longing for peace and happiness but unsettled by the pluralist ethos around us, people today pursue their spiritual journey but find themselves afraid to plant their feet firmly anywhere. While en route they move from belief to belief, often with little other foundation than the assumption that the way forward is to grab whatever happens to be the fad of the day. Perhaps yesterday it was transcendental meditation. Maybe right now it's channeling or perhaps the latest Christian "revival." And who knows what tomorrow may bring. But whatever it is, be assured, today's "pilgrims" will be part of it. So we follow the trends through yoga, psychic phonelines, therapeutic touch, the inner voice, and visualization. We borrow from here and there, sampling a smorgasbord that offers tasty morsels ranging from Buddhist wisdom to Jungian psychology, sprinkled with a liberal dose of Christian ideas.

Twenty-three-year-old Cara Seeger of Victoria, Canada, typifies a pattern repeated throughout North America. Cara performs the ceremonial magic of Wicca, reads tarot cards, and practices Buddhism and Taoism. Her rationale? "I believe all attempts of mankind and womankind to reach for the divine are valid."[8] To many people, the search for meaning through adherence to the "one true faith" is passé. What is "in" is the quest for spirituality. And this quest, they claim, may lead through a variety of religious traditions, each of which offers a partial insight.

What advice do contemporary spiritual guides offer to searching souls in a spiritual society? They admonish us to keep in mind that no one belief system holds all the answers, to view each as a way station along the pathway, and to move with the times!

In such a climate, holding firm convictions does seem strangely anachronistic. Belief, understood as knowledge, assent, and trust, appears to run counter to the new spirituality of our day, at least at first glance.

The Quest for Certainty
in a Pluralist Context

Yet, we all "violate" the pluralist agenda all the time. Despite our pragmatic, eclectic impulse, each of us does hold certain convictions about such "big picture" issues as the nature of ultimate reality and our place in the universe. Whenever you affirm your position on these questions, you implicitly—and sometimes explicitly—reject other views as at best inferior and possibly even false.

Not only do we at times speak the language of certainty but we also long for some sense of certainty in the midst of the uncertainties of our world. We all raise the crucial questions of human existence: "Why am I here?" "Where are we going?" etc. And we all hunger for compelling answers to our questions.

This unquenchable desire for certainty returns us to the question of believing. In the midst of the pluralism of our world, faith does remain possible. We all need a "world-view"—a coherent set of beliefs through which we are able to make sense out of our world and thereby provide an anchor in the midst of life's uncertainties.

But are all beliefs equal? In the end, does it matter at all *what* we believe?

Is What I Believe Important?

In a pluralistic age, belief is "in." This is a good thing. Indeed, an important contribution of our pluralist context has been its reaffirmation of the importance of believing. Yet, many voices assert that it really doesn't make any difference *what* you believe so long as you believe something—anything. Therefore, we ask, "Do beliefs matter at all? Is what you believe important?"

In a word, the answer is yes.

Faith Commitments Affect How We Live

One day Betty (the lead personality of the comic strip that bears her name) was walking through the mall with her friend Alex. Alex was musing about life. In the ensuing soliloquy she noted that she simply thinks too much. How had she come to this conclusion? By observing that the happiest people she knows are the ones who don't seem to think much at all. And why are they happy? Her answer was simple. People who don't think are free to act in whatever way they find personally pleasing. Thinking, in contrast, leads to confusion and second-guessing oneself, so that in the end a person doesn't act at all.

Alex put her finger on an important aspect of human existence: What we think—that is, our belief structure—is important. Why? Because we live out our beliefs. We give evidence of our convictions in what we do. What Alex failed to notice, however, is that we cannot escape from thinking—or believing. We cannot decide to avoid the process altogether. In fact, her conclusion that persons who don't think are free to act in any way that pleases them couches a belief system. It arises out of certain convictions about the nature of reality and what it means to be human.

We all have beliefs. And the fundamental convictions we embrace about the nature of reality shape our conduct. I would dare say that if I were to follow you around for a couple of days, I could soon pinpoint the basic convictions you hold. Oh, not the beliefs you give lip service to, but the fundamental credo that informs what you do.

Take as an example our relationships with one another. Suppose that you perceive the world (or whatever you think stands behind the world) as ultimately capricious, unfaithful, and untrustworthy. This belief may incline you to unfaithfulness in your various relations with others. Suppose further that you believe a human being is ultimately a solitary ego and that rather than an essential aspect of "you" the body is primarily a "pleasure machine." This conviction might just predispose you to look at others largely as prospective sexual partners and to engage in promiscuous sexual practices without much concern about whether you are hurting someone else in the process.

On the other hand, suppose you believe that God is eternally faithful to a creation that is the product of God's hand. This conviction could motivate you to value faithfulness in your relations with others. Suppose you believe that to be human means to live in relationships that foster mutuality, reciprocity, and the coincidence of give and take. And suppose you are convinced that fulfilling another while being fulfilled by that person lies at the heart of human existence. If you are married, such convictions offer a strong motivation to practice marital fidelity.

Beliefs are important. They are crucial if for no other reason than that they determine how we live.

Faith Commitments in Times of Crisis

One dimension of living, however, is especially crucial. What I have said throughout this chapter points to the fact that beliefs take on added importance in the crises of life. Indeed, coping well in the midst of an uncertain world can only happen when we are upheld by beliefs that are religious in nature.

Recent research confirms this conclusion. Several health care studies have determined a connection between belief and personal well-being. For example, at a meeting in 1996 of the American Association for the Advancement of Science, Dr. Dale Matthews of Georgetown University declared, "I believe that physicians can and should encourage patients' autonomous religious activities." Matthews cited studies indicating that religion is beneficial in dealing with drug abuse, alcoholism, depression, cancer, high blood pressure, and heart disease.[9] One specific project suggested that—in the words of Dr. Harold Koenig of Duke University Medical Center—"people who attend church are both physically healthier and less depressed."[10]

In another study of elderly patients undergoing heart surgery researchers determined that patients without religious beliefs had a death rate nearly three times that of religious persons. The leader of the study, Dr. Thomas Oxman, a psychiatrist at Dartmouth Medical School, observed: "It seems that being able to give meaning to a precarious, life-threatening situation— having faith there is some greater meaning or force at work— is medically helpful." On the other hand, "if you can't make sense of what's going on, it's much harder to bear."[11]

The study concluded, however, that neither frequency of participation in religious services nor merely "feeling deeply religious" was the determining factor. Instead, according to Oxman, the crucial aspect was the presence of a set of beliefs in which the patient was able to find solace. Or to cite psychologist David Wulff, what makes the difference is "the sheer optimism or hopefulness that's part of the religious outlook."[12]

Studies such as these suggest that each of us must come to grips with the crucial, existential question: What fundamental beliefs about God, the world, and your place in the cosmos will sustain you when the inevitable crises come your way? What will happen to you, when the storms of life break upon you?

As a multitude of testimonies confirm, in the hour of crisis it is too late to search out a sustaining belief system. When crisis hits, you will grasp whatever convictions you have been forming throughout your life. Will the beliefs which now inform the way you are living be capable of sustaining you in the time of darkness? Can you say with confidence that your beliefs will weather the storm? Can you declare with the old gospel hymn writer:

> Leaning, leaning,
> Safe and secure from all alarms;
> Leaning, leaning,
> Leaning on the everlasting arms.[13]

Many people testify to the sustaining power they have gained through religious faith. One example is that of Ralph Powell, who taught theology in a small midwestern seminary. During the 1970s, Professor Powell watched helplessly as his wife Dorothy lost a long, painful battle against cancer. Shortly after her death he confided to one of his students that sometimes he felt so numb that he could no longer sense God's presence. But then he added that even though the feeling was absent, he knew God was there, sustaining and supporting him. Why? Because the beliefs about God he had come to accept over many years had ingrained in him a confidence that the God in whom he believed would never forsake him, even in his darkest hour. Dr. Powell's belief system provided the foundation he needed to find the way through the fog.

Faith in a Hopeless World

Edvard Munch first exhibited his famous painting *The Scream* in Berlin in 1893. Art critics, however, found the work scandalous. The bleak, agonizing figure depicted in the painting was alien to the naturalistic sensitivities of nineteenth-century viewers. More than a century later, however, Munch's painting has come to rival the *Mona Lisa* as the most reproduced work of art ever created. *The Scream* has found its way into cartoons, posters, advertising materials, mugs, T-shirts, mouse pads, inflatable dolls, beer bottles, and night-lights.

Why? Michael Parke-Taylor, curator of a major Munch exhibit at the Art Gallery of Ontario, provides the clue. *The Scream,* he notes, stands as *the* "image of modern man—totally stressed out and angst-ridden."[14] The forlorn figure has become so popular because people today see their own faces mirrored in the face on Munch's painting.

As the popularity of Munch's "image of modern man" indicates, you and I are living in tumultuous times. Ours is an era of pessimism and despair. How can we find hope in the midst of the uncertainties of our day? The place to begin is with the beliefs we hold on to—or which have the capacity to hold on to us. The task we face is to discover a belief system that can shed light on our world and thereby can illumine our way through the night.

But we must choose wisely. The answer does not lie in belief itself. Nor can we simply pick a set of convictions willy-nilly from among the current options. Why? This takes us back to the intellectual dimension of faith. Faith involves personal trust, to be sure. But such trust must arise from knowledge and assent. Remember what I said earlier about faith including the affirmation about what is true apart from my affirming it? Only if our trust is the outworking of knowledge about what is in fact true about God, the universe, and ourselves can we find true hope in the midst of despair. Ultimately, what we need is to be linked to something—Someone!—bigger than ourselves.

Where can we find this kind of foundation for life? Where can we discover beliefs that bring us genuine hope, because they arise from the One who is true?

To answer this question we must note where beliefs come from. Contemporary sociologists have discovered that what we hold to be true does not arise in a vacuum. We gain our fundamental beliefs from a variety of sources. Above all our convictions are related to the way we were socialized, the society in which we live, and what we have come to accept from what others tell us. In short, beliefs arise out of the community in which we participate.

Therefore, our quest for beliefs that can sustain us leads us to search for a community that embodies the answers to life's deepest questions. And where can I find such a community of faith?

Simply stated the answer is: within the fellowship of believing Christians, the church of Jesus Christ.

The story of a Vancouver teenager, Robyn Clements, offers a helpful example. Although still in her teens, Robyn came to the point where she realized she needed to turn her life around. At first, she thought that in her own strength she could forsake the unwholesome activities that were consuming her life. But after repeated failure, she concluded that she simply did not have the resources within herself to accomplish this task.

One Sunday Robyn found her way into our evening worship service. "When I left the church that evening," she later reported, "I knew there had been a major change in my belief." This marked the turning point in her life. Since then, to cite her own words, "Jesus has given me so much—a new life, renewed hope, and an ability to live."

People today—you and I—are on a spiritual quest. Christians readily admit that they do not have all the answers. But we believe we have found where to look: We boldly suggest that the answers people today are seeking are capsulated in the central convictions of the Christian community.

To these foundational Christian beliefs about human existence we now turn our attention.

NOTES

1. See Lewis Carroll, *Through the Looking Glass and What Alice Found There* (New York: Random House, 1946), 76.
2. See *Fides,* in Richard A. Muller, *Dictionary of Latin and Greek Theological Terms* (Grand Rapids: Baker, 1985), 115–16.
3. See, for example, John Naisbitt and Patricia Aburdene, *Megatrends 2000: Ten New Directions for the 1990s* (New York: Avon Books, 1990), 295–96.

4. Sharon Doyle Driedger, "On a Higher Plane," *Maclean's* 108, no. 52 (Dec. 25, 1995–Jan. 1, 1996): 23.
5. Martin Wroe, "American Pie in the Sky," *Third Way* 18, no. 7 (September 1995): 13.
6. Remi de Roo, bishop in Victoria, B.C., as cited in Peter C. Newman, "New Age Dreams in Hard Times," *Maclean's* 107, no. 41 (October 10, 1994): 38.
7. "Bible Illegal, Man Claims," *The Vancouver Sun* (November 24, 1995): A3.
8. Driedger, "On a Higher Plane," 23.
9. "Going to Church Good for Health, Studies Show," *The Vancouver Sun* (February 12, 1996): A9.
10. "Going to Church," A9.
11. Daniel Goleman, "Researchers Link Faith and Health," *The Vancouver Sun* (February 25, 1995): D11.
12. "Researchers Link Faith and Health," D11.
13. Elisha A. Hoffman, "Leaning on the Everlasting Arms," 1887.
14. Barbara Wickens, ed., "You *Scream, I Scream* . . . ," *Maclean's* 110, no. 9 (March 3, 1997): 14.

Chapter 2
Who Am I and Why Am I Here?

O ne day the German philosopher Arthur Schopenhauer was strolling along the sidewalk. Engrossed in his own reflections, he inadvertently bumped into another pedestrian. "Who do you think you are?" challenged his victim. The angry rhetorical question only plunged the gloomy thinker deeper into the melancholy that plagued him. "Who am I? How I wish I knew," he mused wistfully.

Mary, a successful professional in her late thirties, had taken a leave of absence to attend seminary, where she expected to find answers to the gnawing questions that kept emerging within her. At one point in her struggle, she requested an appointment with me. Thirty minutes into the session she blurted out, holding back the tears: "I no longer know who I really am. And I am afraid that if I find out, there won't be a place for me."

Unlike Schopenhauer, most of us don't spend our waking moments lost in philosophical reflection. Nor do we necessarily come face-to-face with a dramatic crisis of identity as Mary did. Nevertheless, each of us faces the formidable task of finding who we are. We all share the struggle that humans in every generation encounter, the struggle to determine our identity. In fact, we might say that what marks us as humans is our common attempt to gain a sense of personhood. Therefore, the foundational question we all face and to which we must find an answer is: Who am I, and why am I here?

For most of us, "Who am I?" is the first crucial question we encounter when we begin to grapple with the meaning of life. Despite the amount of time and energy we devote to it, we never seem to move beyond this question. Rather than devising a final response to our foundational query, at best we are able to formulate only a provisional answer—an answer that allows us to get on with our lives to a greater or lesser extent and facilitates us in bringing some sense of coherence to the seemingly chaotic life we live.

The question, Who am I? is related to a more general human query. Collectively we wonder, Who are we as humans? And what possible reason—if any—might there be for our presence on planet Earth? My task in this chapter is to explore the Christian response to this question of our human identity, which in turn forms the context for making sense out of our individual existence as well. What does the gospel have to say to this crucial question that confronts us all?

Who Are We?

You and I are not the first humans to wonder, Who am I and why am I here? Sages in every culture since ancient times have pondered this question. Their deliberations invariably led them to consider what it means to be human. Following their example, let us launch an attempt to discover what it means to be human: Who are we as human beings?

When we raise the question, Who are we? we are not looking for a scientific account of human origins or of our common human makeup. Instead, what we really want to know is whether there is anything special about being human. "Who are we?" in other words, is fundamentally a religious question.

What Does It Mean to Be Human?

Does anything set us apart from the rest of the universe? When we ask the question in this manner, we are immediately confronted with the possibility that the answer is no. Our search for what it means to be human might lead to the conclusion that ultimately there is nothing particularly special about us. Indeed, various voices today draw just such a conclusion.

The Human Animal. For some, the question, Who am I? nets a quite simple answer. In their estimation, our truthful response can only be, "I am one living creature among many."

This thinking sometimes surfaces in the contemporary animal rights movement, to cite one example. Some activists conclude that only a vision that places us squarely within the animal realm can provide the antidote for the hubris that leads humans to misuse other living creatures. In their estimation, so long as we perpetuate lofty claims about some supposed higher human status, we will continue to see animals merely as means to our ends, rather than as creatures with inherent dignity. The only way we can come to live appropriately, they assert, is by realizing that humans are but one species among many.

The idea that humans are best understood through our connection to other animals is also prevalent in certain scientific circles. One especially prominent understanding arises out of what is often called "sociobiology."

Sociobiologists assert that all human conduct is rooted in our biological inheritance. Hence, Harvard zoologist Edward O. Wilson describes sociobiology as "the systematic study of the biological basis of all forms of social behavior in all kinds of organisms, including man."[1] Above all, humans are like all other creatures from the simplest to the most complex in that the goal of each is to reproduce as many offspring as possible. The drive to fulfill this goal—this "reproductive imperative"[2]—sociobiologists theorize, influences behavior patterns in all species, whether they be mosquito, monkey, or man.

On this basis, a group of theorists known as "evolutionary psychologists" suggest that the goal of getting one's genes into the next generation lies behind the development of the human mind. They build from the insights of sociobiology to explain certain psychological aspects of life. For example, according to evolutionary psychologists, the immense joy of parental love is due to the fact that offspring carry our genes into posterity. Conversely, a host of neuroses that lead to maladies ranging from suicide to homicide are the result of the mismatch between our minds, designed as they were for life in the ancestral environment of the hunter-gatherer society, and the modern world we now inhabit. Proponents of this "mismatch theory" see in it the explanation for the pervasive sense of discontent that characterizes modern experience.[3]

The Human Computer. While not losing the similarities between humans and other living beings, other theorists are convinced that humans are far more complex and complicated than any other species. These thinkers suggest that a more promising point of comparison in our quest to understand who we are lies in artificial intelligence. In this manner, the question, Who am I? nets the answer, "I am a sophisticated machine."

Such an answer is readily visible in the repeated attempts today to draw models from computer technology to theorize how humans function. Some scientists suggest that the behavior of every organism (including humans) is determined by its genetic structure. They anticipate that once we fully map a creature's DNA instruction tape (including our human DNA), we will gain nearly complete understanding of its repertoire of behaviors, as if it were a computerized automaton.[4]

Other theorists are less inclined to look to DNA as a mechanism that runs the human machine. Instead, they focus attention on the human brain, proposing similarities between it and computer technology. Indeed, in day-to-day life we often speak of the brain as a computer.

More importantly, however, scientists have established an actual dialogue between a nerve cell and a pair of silicon chips. In this experiment, a first chip induced the electrochemical changes that trip the cell's mechanism for inaugurating a nerve-to-nerve signal, and a second chip, in turn, was able to sense this signal. On the basis of this result, several scientists now wonder if beneath the seemingly chaotic exterior, humans are simply sophisticated machines. In the words of one commentator, this development "hints at the strangely regular clockwork behind the mask, the definable nature of the biological machinery that underlies the vagaries of human behavior."[5]

Scientific work such as this is moving toward the possibility of a marriage between neurons and transistors. Some futurists anticipate a day when silicon chips are planted in the human cortex, uniting mind and machine directly, and thereby creating the bionic human.

Not surprisingly, these possibilities repeatedly become fodder for science fiction exploration. For example, the various incarnations of the popular television series *Star Trek* have raised the possible connection between humans and artificial intelligence, especially computers. A fascinating subplot of *Star Trek: The Next Generation* that intrigued vast audiences from 1987 to 1994 moves a giant step beyond the wedding of brain and computer chip to the humanization of the computer itself. The highly intelligent and curious android, Data, desired not only to learn what it means to be human but in fact to become human. As the series unfolded, Data increasingly took on the human characteristics that he lacked—a sense of humor, emotion, the ability to dream, and even the experience of intimacy.

The less popular fourth series, *Star Trek: Voyager*, that aired in the 1990s included a similar narrative line. This time, the ship's doctor, a computer program that included a holographic image, took on increasingly human characteristics in a similar manner to his android predecessor. In addition, there were those intriguing antagonists, the Borg, who repeatedly arose in the later *Star Trek* series, including the movie *First Contact*. As the name itself suggested, derived as it was from the word *cyborg*, the Borg were a race of artificial intelligence who sought to assimilate every culture that came across their collective path.

The message of this recurring theme is the same: Humans are not dissimilar from "artificial intelligence." Who am I? I am fundamentally a sophisticated computer.

The Immortal Soul. Despite the pull of viewpoints that are content to describe humans either as animals intent on getting

DNA into the next generation or as sophisticated, intelligent machines, most people remain unconvinced that these suggestions exhaust what it means to be human. There must be more to the human person.

But what is this "more"? Some look to the idea of the "soul" for a clue. Who am I? They answer, "I am an immortal soul temporarily housed in a body."

The suggestion that to be human means being an immortal soul boasts a long historical pedigree. In the Western tradition, this idea dates at least to the Greek philosopher Plato (428–348 B.C.E.). The ancient thinker believed that lying beyond the physical, temporal world of sense experience is an eternal realm of pure, unchangeable essences (the "forms"). Humans, he theorized, belong to eternity, for the goal of our existence is to know and contemplate the forms. Our true nature is connected with this contemplative purpose. Each of us is ultimately an immortal soul.

Plato's focus on the eternal realm of the forms carried far-reaching implications for life in the body. Rather than assisting us in fulfilling our lofty purpose, the Greek philosopher taught, the body in which we now find ourselves is actually a hindrance. It impedes us from clear contemplation. Consequently, the goal of life is to leave the body behind. Only as disembodied souls are we fully able to know the eternal forms in their purity.

Although Plato lived twenty-three centuries ago, his ideas continue to exercise a strong influence today. Many people who are convinced that humans are somehow special resort to Plato's language of the "immortal soul" to explain our human uniqueness. The essential "me," they declare, is the immortal soul within.

Some even go beyond Plato and, borrowing ideas from Eastern religious traditions, link the soul with the divine. Actress Shirley MacLaine, for example, once reported that she takes five minutes each day to remind herself of her fundamental divinity. Why? Because of the power that words carry:

> Affirmations are spoken resolutions which, when used properly, align the physical, mental, and spiritual energies. The

ancient Hindu vedas claimed that the spoken words *I am*, or *Aum* in Hindu, set up a vibrational frequency in the body and mind which align the individual with his or her higher self and with the God-source.[6]

Despite its perennial popularity, the suggestion that being human means having (or being) an immortal soul suffers from two debilitating difficulties. First, it assumes that immortality is something we possess individually and within ourselves. The phrase itself, "immortal soul," suggests this, for it attributes immortality directly to the soul. In keeping with this understanding, many people assume that there is something inside them that continues to live, even after death. Indeed, in their understanding it is not the person but merely the body that dies.

Contrary to what the language of "immortal soul" suggests, however, there is nothing within us that is intrinsically immortal; there is no aspect of our being to which we can without reservation attribute immortality. We simply don't have within ourselves the power to live forever. Rather than a prerogative we possess, life is a gift we receive. Beginning in the womb and throughout our days on Earth, we are dependent on others for our ongoing existence.

This is obviously the case with our biological existence, but it is evident in the nonphysical aspects of life as well. For this reason, we often speak about those things—from culture to friendship—that nurture the human spirit. In short, we are dependent creatures in the entirety of our being. There is simply no aspect of our personal existence that is self-sustaining. Aware of this, Christians declare that life in all its dimensions, including our hope for everlasting life, is God's gracious gift to us.

Second, the claim that each of us is an immortal soul may actually hide too narrow an understanding of immortality. This view of humanness assumes that immortality is the exclusive property of the soul to the exclusion of the body. In the end, only the soul is immortal. Like Plato, proponents envision the soul eventually shedding the body. When this occurs, they add, the soul finds its true home and is finally able to fulfill its true purpose.

Inherent in the belief that we are immortal souls is a duality (a separation or division) between soul and body, and in turn between what we perceive to be immaterial and the physical. Rather than the two aspects of the duality being equal, the declaration "We are immortal souls" almost inevitably elevates the soul above the body, and the immaterial above the physical. If the true "me" is the soul and not the body, then rather than being part of who I really am, my physical body is little more than a shell that encases for a time the real "me" residing inside.

Shirley MacLaine's description of her supposedly "out-of-body" experience provides a case in point:

> Had my spiritual energy separated itself from the physical form? Was I floating *as* my soul? I was consciously aware of my questions as I soared freely above the Earth. I was so conscious of what I felt that in those moments I understood how irrelevant my physical body was.[7]

Think of the implications of this: If my body is not truly "me"—if it doesn't belong to the "me" that lives forever—then what the body desires or even does is quite unimportant. If the physical aspect of earthly existence is only temporal in contrast to the eternal dimension connected with the soul, then I need not be concerned about the physical.

From this understanding, some people conclude that we ought to ignore or even seek to escape from the physical, bodily aspects of life. More widespread today, however, is the exact opposite conclusion. Because the body is not an essential part of who I am, many people assert, I can "indulge the body." I can engage in bodily desires with little or no restraint. Taken to an extreme, this view transforms the body into merely a temporal "pleasure machine." This is especially evident in the contemporary attitude that views sex as primarily an activity that we engage in—or even a means for the expression of personal freedom—rather than an aspect of who we are and hence expressive of our innermost being.

Being Human Means
Being an Embodied Person

There is yet a fourth possible answer to the question of our human nature. This response maintains a special place for humankind while avoiding the dangers connected with speaking about an immortal soul. Who am I? "I am an embodied person."

This answer arises from two important aspects of Christian teaching. First, Christians believe that God *created* us as embodied beings. This idea is evident in the creation narratives in the opening chapters of the Bible. In the first story, God creates humankind to be an integral part of the material world. The second narrative offers more detail. God forms Adam from the dust of the ground (material) and breathes life into him. As a result, Adam is an embodied being, a material creature animated by the life principle from God.

The declaration that we are embodied persons arises secondly from the Christian hope of resurrection.

To understand what this event will be like we must look to the resurrected Jesus. The various New Testament portrayals of the risen Lord all assert the same point: The one who appeared to the disciples on numerous occasions was none other than the prophet from Nazareth who had been crucified. Through resurrection he was transformed into the fullness of eternal life; nevertheless, the risen Jesus remained an embodied being. Jesus' disciples touched him, ate with him, and conversed with him. And they knew who he was, for he was recognizable by those who had known him.

Following the New Testament, Christians believe that we will one day participate in the same resurrection Jesus experienced. Like his, our resurrection will involve the body. Hence, the doorway to eternity is not the soul shedding the body and thereby becoming its true self. On the contrary, we enter eternity only through the transformation of our entire person as the embodied beings we are.

Why Are We Here?

We have offered a first response to our common human query. Who am I?—"I am an embodied person." But our quest to understand what it means to be human involves a second aspect as well. It looks beyond who we are as such to the purpose of our existence. We also wonder, "Why am I here?"

Even Charlie Brown has been known to raise this question. One night the poor fellow was in bed suffering from insomnia. Speaking to no one in particular, he mused about how he sometimes lies awake at night asking the age-old question "Why am I here?" After a pause, the melancholy boy then explained that an unknown voice from out of the blue responds to his query by inquiring as to where he in fact wants to be.

Contrary to the mock-serious response of the unknown voice, the search to discover our human purpose is crucial. Raising this question launches us again on what is fundamentally a religious quest.

The Homeless Human

Why are we here? What is our purpose? In the modern era, people have tended to find the answer in our human ability to act as "creators." Modern humans view the universe largely as the material for our creative and transforming activity. We sense that in itself the world is not a hospitable place. As a result, we perceive our human task to be that of fashioning a place for ourselves out of whatever we find around us. We desire to make a "home" for ourselves within what is otherwise an unfriendly universe.

Whenever we speak about "raw materials" or "natural resources" we show how much a part of our common vocabulary this modern outlook is. And we repeatedly find the modern ethos expressed in "pop" culture. The old *Star Trek* television series offers a typical example. The program's dictum sounded the pervasive modernist note. The human task is to explore our "world"—of which space now looms as "the final frontier"—and to harness the knowledge gained through such exploration for human benefit. In short, in the minds of the creators of the series, space exploration—epitomized in the voyages of the Enterprise—serves the wider task of creating a "home" for humankind in the universe.

One especially illustrative episode ("Devil in the Dark") took place on a lonely planet that humans had colonized for the sake of mining a highly useful mineral ("pergium"). However, an alien creature who lived deep beneath the surface was sabotaging the mining operations. She had even killed several colonists. Just before the TV hour elapsed, the efforts of strong leadership (Kirk), superior intellect (Spock), and medical science (McCoy) saved the day. Together this trio of heroes found a win-win solution. The human colonists would live together with the indigenous "Horta," each side leaving the other alone. But better yet, because the Horta tunnel through rock, this peaceful coexistence would actually increase the production of the mine.

The appeal of the modern ethos is strengthened by its apparent foundation in certain theories propagated by the modern human sciences. One important theory comes from biology. In contrast to animals, which are bound to their world by limitations set by heredity, humans are characterized by what one biologist calls "plasticity and adaptability." This endowment enables us to alter and even control our environment to an extent unparalleled among the animals.[8] But adaptability has a "downside" as well. In contrast to other species, each of which has a discernable "niche" within an ordered biological framework, biologists have yet to discover a set role for humankind that can explain our purpose for existence.

In addition to our adaptability, we are uniquely gifted with "self-transcendence," the ability to stand back from ourselves. We can place ourselves "above" the here-and-now and thereby scrutinize ourselves. At the same time, we enjoy the unique possibility of continually experiencing our environment in new ways. We can envision an existence "beyond" any "world" we create. But this too has its negative side, for it leads to a "homelessness" or "restlessness." We are never completely fulfilled by any one "world" we fashion for ourselves. Instead, we continually chase an illusive "something" that surpasses the here-and-now.

No wonder a growing chorus of voices is now calling for a revisioning of the modern attitude toward the world around us. The emerging postmodern ethics is looking for a new understanding of ourselves that would see humans not as separate and above, but as an integral part of the environment from which we live. But even a revised understanding does not provide an answer to our quest for purpose. The question still remains, Why are we here?

We Are to Be God's Image-Bearers

You and I are not the first humans to wonder, Why am I here? What is our human purpose? Long before Jesus was born, the Hebrew sages raised this question. For example, after contemplating the vastness and majesty of the universe, the psalmist declared in amazement, "What are human beings that you are mindful of them, mortals that you care for them?" (Ps. 8:4). The ancient thinker then offered a response to the perplexing question about the purpose of our existence: "You have made them a little lower than God and crowned them with glory and honor. You have given them dominion over the works of your hands; you have put all things under their feet" (Ps. 8:5–6).

The declaration from the pen of the sage echoed the words that stand at the climax of the creation story in the opening chapter of Genesis: "So God created humankind in his image, in the image of God he created them; male and female he created them" (Gen. 1:27).

As these ancient writings indicate, our purpose is to be God's image-bearers. What does this mean?

Dominion. Our first response may be to connect the image of God with exercising "dominion" over creation. According to the first creation story, God's intention to make human beings in the divine image included that they "have dominion over the fish of the sea, and over the birds of the air, and over the cattle and over all the wild animals of the earth, and over every creeping thing that creeps upon the earth" (Gen. 1:26). In keeping with this understanding, the psalmist concluded, "You have given them dominion over the works of your hands; you have put all things under their feet" (Ps. 8:6).

Unfortunately, many people read these texts through modern eyes. They see in "dominion" the idea that nature around us exists solely for our benefit and our refashioning. These ancient texts, they conclude, provide license for exploiting the world around us.

In a certain sense, being God's image-bearers does entail dominion over the earth. But the point of the ancient texts is quite different from what the modern view suggests. The kings of the ancient Near East often left images of themselves in those cities or territories where they could not be present in person. Such images served to represent the kings' majesty and power.[9] In a similar manner, God placed humankind upon Earth to represent the Creator.[10] Thus, our purpose is to show to all creation what God is like, especially as we mirror the divine character. As we care for creation after the manner of the Creator, we exercise true "dominion" in accordance with the purpose for our existence.

Community. But what is the divine character? As we will develop more fully in chapter 4, the God whom Christians proclaim is characterized by love, because this God is triune—the Father, Son, and Holy Spirit united in love. Consequently, to be the image of God means to reflect the divine love. Because God is this eternal fellowship, we reflect God's character in fellowship with one another. Hence, our purpose as humans involves living in fellowship or fostering "community."

By suggesting that humans in relationship with one another reflect the divine character and hence are the image of God, the creation stories highlight the social nature of our human purpose. Thus, in the first narrative after declaring, "Let us make humankind in our image" (Gen. 1:26), the Creator fashions humankind as male and female (Gen. 1:27). The story of Adam and Eve in Genesis 2 deepens this theme. God creates the female to deliver the male from his isolation. This primal community of man and woman then produces offspring, from which eventually emerges human society.

What began in the Garden of Eden finds its completion at the end of history. The final book in the Bible envisions a day when humans will enjoy perfect fellowship—complete community—in the new creation (Rev. 22:1–4).

As we live in love—that is, as we give expression to true community—we reflect the character of the Creator. And as we reflect God's love, we also live in accordance with our own true nature. Only by being persons-in-community do we find our true identity—that form of the "world" in which we are truly "at home."

Jesus articulated this truth in his astonishing statement: "For those who want to save their life will lose it, and those who lose their life for my sake will find it" (Matt. 16:25). The way to true life entails giving one's life in relationship to him. In other words, we find our true identity only as we participate together in the community of Christ's followers. In so doing, we bring honor to our Creator, for we reflect the very character of God.

Implications of the Image of God. Acknowledging that our human purpose is to live as the image of God carries great implications. For starters, it gives meaning to life.

People today are frantically searching—hoping to bring some meaning into their fragmented and frantic existence. The good news of the Christian gospel, however, is that our lives *already* have meaning. God has created us for a purpose, namely, to glorify God and to enjoy God forever—to allude to the words of the Westminster Catechism.[11] We exist in order to reflect God's character, to be God's image-bearers.

Therefore, our lives need not remain the meaningless collections of unrelated events they so often appear to be. On the contrary, the various dimensions of our existence can be fitted together into a meaningful whole. The pattern whereby we can weave the aspects of our lives together lies in the goal, the purpose, or the destiny God intends for us. As we seek to be God's image-bearers a fundamental unity begins to emerge in the day-to-day experience of living in God's world.

Further, acknowledging that our human purpose is to be God's image-bearers leads us to view all creatures as valuable. But in saying this, we must avoid falling into the widely held idea that we are the ones who determine the value of others. Their value does not arise from their utility for us. They are not valuable insofar as they serve our ends. Instead, all creatures are valuable because God values them. And the loving Creator desires that we show God's own loving character—divine love—toward all creatures.

In the same manner, the realization that we are to be God's image-bearers leads us to view all humans as valuable. God has created each one for the same purpose, namely, to enter into relationships that show forth the divine character. Knowing this, we honor all human beings as having divinely endowed worth.

What Has Gone Wrong?

Who am I? I am an embodied person.

Why am I here? To be a person whose relationships show God's own loving character.

That may be who God intends me to be. But the sad fact is, this lofty purpose and the reality I experience are poles apart. True, I sometimes seem to do loving acts. Yet, regardless of how good I may appear on the surface, deep inside I know I am self-centered and mean-spirited. Despite moments of genuine altruism, I know that most of the time I am busily promoting myself at the expense of others. So often I maliciously seek to destroy what others have constructed. And I am part of a people who plunder the good earth that nourishes us all.

Obviously something has gone wrong. But what?

The Nature of Our Problem

Taking our cue from what we have said about our human purpose we might pinpoint our problem as "failure." Simply stated, we fail to be the divine image-bearers we were created to be.

We display this failure in many ways. It is present in our quarreling with one another and our misuse of creation. It permeates our passive apathy toward God, others, and the world entrusted to our care. This suggests that our failure is above all a failure of relationship. Rather than living in wholesome relationships that reflect the divine character (love), we know only brokenness.

This breakdown of relationships is captured in the word *alienation*. Indeed, many people today know alienation firsthand. Within their hearts is a gnawing sense that they are separated from all that is really important. Yet they also genuinely desire "connection."

For example, an entire generation is reaching adulthood without a sense of being connected to the traditional sources of relationship, such as strong family ties. This is evident in the changing settings of the most popular "sitcoms" of the day. In the 1950s, prime-time television programs featured intact families (*The Adventures of Ozzie and Harriet, Father Knows Best, Leave It to Beaver*) or at least supportive extended families (*The Andy Griffith Show, My Three Sons*). By the 1990s, in contrast, the traditional family had disappeared. Families portrayed in the newer programs were more likely than not to be dysfunctional (*The Simpsons, Married . . . with Children*), and many programs didn't include families at all. Instead, they looked to friendship circles as the source of support and care (*Seinfeld, Friends*). Why are these programs so popular? Because in the experience of an increasing number of people the traditional family either doesn't exist at all or what does exist of it has actually become a source of alienation.

Alienation arises from another, perhaps even unexpected source as well—technology. Despite all the great promises about how technology would enhance our lives, our technological society has come to be characterized by an increased sense of alienation. For example, an evening together, which in the past was marked by conversation or cooperative work on a project, today often consists in nothing more engaging than watching television in the same room. Many people now find spending a hour in an internet "chat room" far easier than conversing with people who are physically present.

Technological advances also have fostered a sense of alienation from creation. As food production has become increasingly mechanized, most people have lost all real day-to-day ties to the "natural" environment and its role in sustaining human life. Indeed, the only contact the vast majority of North Americans have with animals is either by owning house pets or visiting zoos.

In so many ways we sense alienation from one another and from creation. Christians declare, however, that our root human problem lies deeper. Above all we are alienated from our Creator. And this fundamental disconnectedness lies at the root of other dimensions of our sensed alienation.

The narrative of the Garden of Eden in the opening chapters of the Bible indicates that we were created to enjoy perfect fellowship with God. But instead of basking in the divine presence, we flee from God. Presuming that God is hostile toward us, we project our enmity toward God on God. In fear, we run from the only One who can overcome our fear, brokenness, and hostility. We seek to escape from the only One who can fulfill our deepest needs.

This broken relationship with God leads, in turn, to alienation in other directions. Instead of enjoying wholesome, enriching relationships with one another, we exploit one another. We jostle with one another for power, influence, and prominence. Or we allow others to rob us of our dignity and sense of worth.

Likewise, rather than living as divinely mandated stewards of creation, we view the world as a storehouse of natural resources that exists to serve our wants. We no longer interact with the earth as an organic whole that we manage on God's behalf. Instead, in our insatiable but misguided quest for a "home," we view creation as the raw material for our industrious activity or as an untamed foe that we must conquer. As a result, creation itself now groans, awaiting its liberation—to allude to the words of the apostle Paul (Rom. 8:19–22).

Our alienation from God also works its way into our individual, personal lives. We sense that we are alienated from our selves, that we are our worst enemies. Even more significantly, we know we are not living according to our purpose for existence. As a result, we sense within ourselves a festering alienation from our true nature.

The Extent of Our Problem

How deep does this human failure lie in our being?

Many people believe that our human problem, while critical, is nevertheless circumstantial. As a result, they are convinced that we can "fix" our broken condition ourselves. These people may differ about what the proper cure entails, but they agree that the medicine is readily at hand. As a result, they set out on a quest for some aspect of human life untainted by the consequences of sin.

Human Self-Help Programs. In the modern era, some physicians of the human condition looked to reason for the key to solving our problem. They suggested that in the end our human problem is largely due to ignorance and superstition. Therefore, the way forward was through education.

Lying behind this view was the assumption that each of us has a treasure store (rationality) within, waiting to be developed. If we could simply develop our keen innate powers of observation and deduction we could find the answers we need. Thus, if each of us became a Sherlock Holmes in our own sphere of living, proponents theorized, we would soon discover that what appears on the surface to be a great mystery is in the end merely "elementary." As a result, the modern era was an individualistic and optimistic era. It focused on the "self-made" man and assumed the inevitability of progress, all based on the faulty conjecture that our powers of reason were unaffected by our human failure.

Most people today are less optimistic than their forebears about what humans can accomplish through the careful use of reason. But for many, this only suggests that we should look in some other direction. Consequently, great numbers scurry off to self-help programs and individual or group therapy sessions. They flock to Eastern religious teachers who promise to release a power they claim lies within each of us. Or they gravitate to those Christian churches that promise health, wealth, and success.

The widely held belief that the final answer to our problem lies within was typified in Mariah Carey's early 1990s hit song "Hero." She optimistically announced that each of us could find a hero inside our heart, an answer inside our soul, and an inner strength to carry on, if only we would look hard enough.

Some people, however, have given up on this quest. Their despair leads them to retreat from the world into some supposedly pristine oasis within what they otherwise perceive to be a basically negative or even evil situation. They look to a special realm where they hope to find the purity and innocence so sadly lacking in their everyday world.

Enticed by the media, especially the movie industry, the realm of choice for some people is sex. They believe that if only they were to discover the perfect sexual encounter, for one brief moment they could be transported out of the failure of the present and into the lost Garden of Eden.

Such suggestions may offer a measure of success for a time. Nevertheless, ultimately they are all doomed to fail, simply because they do not take seriously enough the depth of our problem. In the end our human failure is more than an inconsequential defect on the surface of our lives. Something is amiss at the core of our being. The problem lies deep within our personal "control center," the nucleus of our existence, or—to use the biblical language—the human "heart" (Mark 7:14–23; Matt. 12:33–37).

Our Human Heart Problem. In the Bible, Paul described this corruption of the heart in vivid terms. He declares that our "foolish hearts" are "darkened" (Rom. 1:21) and our minds "corrupt"

(1 Tim. 6:5), even hostile to God (Rom. 8:7–8). And Jesus observed that rather than abhorring our situation, we actually *love* darkness instead of light (John 3:19). In fact, so pervasive is this problem that the Bible speaks of us as being enslaved (John 8:34; Rom. 7:21–23). It depicts the brokenness of our situation as an alien, evil force that holds us in its grasp. How ludicrous it appears, then, to expect that by looking within ourselves or by following our reason we can find a solution to our human problem!

But what about "free will"? You might protest against the biblical idea of enslavement, on the basis that we are "free moral agents."

Even though at first glance it may appear to carry the day, this often-voiced protest presupposes an erroneous understanding of "free will." It mistakenly looks to the everyday experience of choosing among alternatives: "Should I wear my black or my brown skirt?" "Should I order the chicken sandwich or the clam chowder?" On the basis of experiences such as these, we picture ourselves as self-motivated choosers who stand before all decisions—whether what we will wear, what we will eat, or how we will live—unencumbered by any overpowering inclination to decide for one option or another.

A growing number of people today, however, are realizing that we don't stand before decisions as neutral choosers. For example, many readily understand the language of enslavement, because they know the stark reality of addictive behavior, whether in the form of substance abuse, a sexual addiction, or the abuse of another person. These people are aware of how someone can so easily become trapped by the "cycle of addiction"—or better stated, the *spiral* of addiction—which draws its prey ever deeper into its grasp. They know as well that at the heart of addiction is a fundamental brokenness of relationship—alienation. And they are aware of how this brokenness in turn leads to further alienation.

But we must take this a step further. Our enslavement to an alien, evil power suggests that our plight is ultimately debilitating. Our innate resources are simply too meager to pull us out of the mire. Why? The answer lies in what we noted earlier about the depth of our human problem. We are not dealing with some mere surface blemish on what is otherwise a beautiful human face. Instead, our failure lies at the very core of our being. As a consequence, the human problem extends to every aspect of our lives. Because there is no dimension of our existence that lies safely beyond its grasp, there is no power within us that we can marshal to gain our liberation.

There is no return to Eden. Not through sex. Not through money. Not through pleasure. Not through "success." And not through the release of some internal power. In the end, when we attempt to latch on to something within ourselves, all we can grab hold of is our own human frailty.

The Responsibility for Our Problem

Many people today readily admit we have a problem. And most quite willingly acknowledge, at least in theory, their own personal shortcomings. Very few, however, readily attach blame to themselves.[12] Instead, we tend to excuse our foibles and even our despicable deeds.

We exonerate ourselves by claiming we are the product of some illness, the treatment we endured as children, the social environment in which we live, or the specific genetic makeup we were handed by our parents. Or we might take solace from those scientists who suggest that the fault lies with evolution: Our human problem is indeed due to the mismatch between the human brain and the contemporary environment. In short, we see ourselves as victims, not perpetrators. And because we are victims, we declare, we bear no responsibility for our human problem.

The biblical writers, however, will not let us off the hook so easily. Not only do we fail to live as we ought, we are responsible for this failure. This unhappy conclusion arises already at the beginning of the biblical story. Indeed, the first question the book of Genesis addresses after speaking about the creation of the universe is "When and how did the human problem arise?" And the answer it gives is simply: at the beginning through a willful human act.

The curtain on the biblical drama opens in the Garden of Eden. According to the story, we began our existence in seemingly perfect innocence. As the divine image-bearers, the first human pair enjoyed fellowship with God (Gen. 3:8), savored transparency with each other (Gen. 2:25), and experienced harmony with all creation (Gen. 2:15–16,19–20).

Despite the bliss of the garden, Adam and Eve plunged humankind into sin (Gen. 3:1–7). This downward plummet began with mistrust. They believed the serpent when he raised subtle doubts about God's goodness. They fell for the trap he set when he held before them the possibility of a heightened knowledge that God supposedly had maliciously reserved for himself. The Genesis story concludes, however, with the sad reality of the consequences of their act (Gen. 3:8–19). Through their disobedience, Adam and Eve destroyed the fellowship with God, each other, and creation that had characterized life in the garden. The idyllic community was shattered. They were banished from paradise (Gen. 3:23), and the principle of death invaded their lives.

But what does this ancient story have to do with us today?

Whatever it may say about the history of Adam and Eve, the Genesis narrative is not merely reporting their personal history. Instead, the story is also about us. It describes a failure in which we all participate. Like Adam and Eve, we too face the choice between trusting obedience and faithless disobedience. Like they, we also readily question God's goodness, and to our detriment we opt for rebellion against God's good purpose for our lives. No wonder we sense alienation at the very core of our being. No wonder we feel the sting of death.

Yet there are certain elements that set our situation apart from that narrated in the text. The first temptation came *to* Adam and Eve, for it was instigated by the serpent. Our plight, in contrast, is internal. We sense the presence of an alien intruder *within* our being. Further, the first failure occurred in a pristine community—in a garden in which our first parents enjoyed fellowship with God, each other, and all creation. We, in contrast, act in the context of prior failure and loss of community. The evil our parents brought into the world carries consequences into the present, for once destroyed, the primordial community remains forever lost. Rather than simply returning to "the beginning," therefore, we have no alternative but to start in the present with the conditions of the world as they now are.

In this sense, the first failure has tainted the world and irreparably altered us, the earth's human inhabitants. No longer do we experience creation, our co-pilgrims, our Creator, or even ourselves as friends. Instead, the pristine community—fellowship without flaws, wholesomeness without a history of hurt—is gone for all time.

At the same time, although the first disobedience decimated the pristine experience of community, in a certain sense we continually repeat the ancient fall. Our attitudes and actions perpetrate the same destruction of fellowship that marked the error of our parents. We continually destroy the semblances of community that here and there emerge among us. Nations break the peace through war. Families quarrel and feud. Marital bliss becomes the casualty of abuse. And the list continues.

Is There Hope?

Who are we and why are we here? We are embodied persons whose purpose is to reflect the character of the Creator in all our relationships, but we are caught in a failure that has characterized human existence since the beginning. Rather than reflecting the divine love, we live in the midst of brokenness. Within ourselves we have no answer to this distressing situation. If there is a solution, it must come from beyond.

Fortunately, the biblical story doesn't end with our sorry plight. It narrates as well the story of a God who suffers our alienation. The Bible depicts the length to which God our Creator has gone to be our Savior as well. But before we can take up that aspect of the narrative, we must turn our attention to two other pressing contemporary questions.

NOTES

1. E. O. Wilson, *On Human Nature,* Bantam Books edition (New York: Bantam Books, 1979), 16–17.
2. See Robert Wallace, *The Genesis Factor* (New York: William Morrow and Co., 1979), 17. Wallace entitles this chapter, "The Reproductive Imperative—or Why You *Really* Love Your Children."
3. Robert Wright, "The Evolution of Despair," *Time* 146, no. 9 (August 28, 1995): 50–56.
4. Nicholas Wade, "Doing the Unthinkable," *The Vancouver Sun* (September 30, 1995): D7.
5. Wade, "Doing the Unthinkable," D7.
6. Shirley MacLaine, *Dancing in the Light* (New York: Bantam, 1985), 118, 120.
7. Shirley MacLaine, *Out on a Limb* (New York: Bantam, 1983), 333.
8. Ashley Montagu, *Man in Process* (New York: Mentor Books, 1961), 17–18.
9. Gerhard von Rad, *"eikon,"* in the *Theological Dictionary of the New Testament,* ed. Gerhard Kittel, trans. Geoffrey W. Bromiley (Grand Rapids: Eerdmans, 1964), 2:392. See also Henri Blocher, *In the Beginning: The Opening Chapters of Genesis,* trans. David G. Preston (Leicester, England: InterVarsity, 1984), 81.
10. Gerhard von Rad, *Genesis,* trans. John H. Marks, in the *Old Testament Library,* ed. G. Ernest Wright (Philadelphia: Westminster, 1972), 58.
11. "The Westminster Shorter Catechism," question 1, in *Creeds of Christendom,* ed. Philip Schaff, three volumes, reprint edition (Grand Rapids: Baker, 1977), 3:676.
12. This was noted over two decades ago. See Karl Menninger, *Whatever Became of Sin?* (New York: Hawthorn Books, 1973).

Chapter 3
Are We Alone in the Universe?

*I*f "Who am I?" is the first existential question we all face as humans, then surely our second query is: Are we alone in the universe?

From ancient times to the present, people in many cultures have posed this question. For example, his musings about human existence led the ancient psalmist to place humans in a world populated by other spiritual beings as well. "What is humankind?" In one translation of the psalmist's words, we are "a little lower than the heavenly beings" (Ps. 8:5, NIV). In saying this, he expressed a belief present in nearly every human society: We are not the only intelligent life-forms in the universe. On the contrary, we are surrounded by "angels."

Is this truly the case? In what sense might we not be alone? Who else is "out there"? Are these "others" friendly? benevolent? good? In short, do angels really exist? And if so, what kind of creatures are they?

The Demise and Return of Angels

Is there anyone out there? Throughout much of the twentieth century people generally assumed that we were alone in the universe. The scientifically oriented mind was averse to accepting without verifiable proof any claim about encounters with alien beings in whatever form. The very idea of purely spiritual beings, ghosts, or aliens "buzzing around" our planet undetected seemed out of sync with an enlightened, rational approach to questions of what is and what is not real. Even the practice of labeling such matters "paranormal" displays a skeptical bias.

The Rejection of Angels. The roots of this suspicious stance lay in the Enlightenment era (roughly the 1600s and 1700s). Before that, people had had a lively, complicated understanding of the spirit world. They believed that angels were everywhere. Specific angels governed the four elements (earth, air, water, and fire) and moved the stars. Each day of the week, season of the year, astrological sign, and hour of the day came under the authority of a corresponding angel.[1] And demons were found everywhere as well.

Enlightenment thinkers rejected this fixation on supernatural beings, regarding it as pure superstition. Even Christian theologians came to find earlier teachings about angels and demons an embarrassment as they attempted to articulate the faith to people enamored with reason and science. The idea that the universe could be populated by such entities seemed out of place in an era in which what is real was defined solely by what could be determined by the scientific method. As theologian Bernard Ramm aptly mused, in such a climate angels seemed "to intrude upon the scene like the unexpected visit of the country relatives to their rich city kinsfolk."[2]

In this task of eliminating supernatural beings from the Western worldview, the Enlightenment rationalists had at their disposal a powerful tool named for the medieval thinker William of Ockham. Simply stated, this methodological dictum, known as "Ockham's razor," asserts that "entities are not to be multiplied beyond necessity."[3] According to this rule, in explaining any phenomenon, we should avoid introducing more principles or more active agents than necessary. That is, we ought to accept the simplest explanation of the data.

Why introduce demon possession, for example, to account for what might just as easily be termed an epileptic fit? Why speak of an angel's intervention, when the avoidance of a possibly fatal accident can be accounted for by known laws of cause and effect?

Rationalist thinkers utilized Ockham's razor to shave off the embarrassing whiskers from the face of the modern understanding of the universe. By eliminating every appeal to an array of supernatural beings, they left us with "normal" explanations for what others thought were "paranormal" or "miraculous" occurrences.

Are we alone in the universe? For all practical purposes, the modern answer tended to be "Yes!" Enlightenment rationalists had become convinced that "nature"—that is, the universe outside the human person—operated according to laws of regularity somewhat akin to a lifeless machine. To date at least, the scientific method had been able to substantiate only one intelligent species in the universe: humankind.

The Renewed Popularity of Angels. Recently, however, the mood has changed dramatically. The possibility that we may not be alone in the universe has captured the imagination of an increasing number of people. Many are now fascinated by the possibility that the universe is populated by hosts of other beings. A Gallup poll in August 1994 indicated that 76 percent of teenagers believe in angels, up from 64 percent in 1968. (A similar poll in 1993 set the figure for adults at 69 percent).[4] These statistics indicate an interesting trend. Just when it seemed that rationalism and science had exorcised the cosmic powers from the Western worldview, angels—whom many thought had been forever discarded in the Enlightenment—have returned en masse.

Time magazine offered this appraisal:

In the past few years [angels] have lodged in the popular imagination, celestial celebrities trailing clouds of glory as they come. There are angels-only boutiques, angel newsletters, angel seminars, angels on *Sonya Live*. A *Time* poll indicates that most Americans believe in angels. Harvard Divinity School has a course on angels; Boston College has two. Bookstores have had to establish angel sections. In the most celebrated play on Broadway, Tony Kushner's Pulitzer-prizewinning *Angels in America,* a divine messenger ministers to a man with AIDS. In *Publishers Weekly*'s religious bestseller list, five of the 10 paperback books are about angels.[5]

All of this points toward a yearning not only to believe that we are not alone but also to make contact with whatever "others" inhabit our universe.

Spacemen, Ghosts, or Heavenly Hosts?

But what are these seemingly mysterious beings? Opinions vary. Some erroneously equate angels with aliens from outer space. Others mistakenly believe spirits of deceased humans now haunt the earth either as angels or demons. Many people prefer the more traditionally Christian view that angels are spiritual messengers from a realm beyond. Let's look more closely at the options proposed today.

Intelligent Species from Outer Space?

It's Wednesday evening at the Omega Centre, Toronto's largest New Age bookstore. In the conference room several dozen people, who have paid $16 each, are attending a session with "trance-channeler" Anne Morse. Tonight Morse is supposedly tuning in to messages from five thousand interplanetary "Transeekers" coming from a cloaked spaceship hovering above the building.

Once Morse was queried about whether she has ever been visited from outer space. The woman responded affirmatively: "from the Pleiades." But then she added, "However, there was no actual physical contact yet."[6]

UFOs and Popular Culture. Widespread interest in other intelligent beings was piqued when the theory of evolution gained broad acceptance in Western culture. The evolutionary hypothesis led many people to conclude that the same processes that gave rise to life on Earth could just as likely be at work elsewhere in the universe. This invited speculation about the potential for the existence of life-forms even more advanced than humans. And wouldn't intelligent life from other realms in the universe eventually discover our planet?

The growing interest in alien visitation caught the imagination of the movie industry. Hollywood churned out a wave of successful films ranging from the philosophical *2001: A Space Odyssey* to the more entertaining and sentimental *ET: The Extra-Terrestrial.* Other media productions, such as the perennially popular *Star Trek* series, took the reverse route, featuring human space explorers on a mission "to seek out new life" and hence to encounter intelligent beings on their home turf. In an interesting twist, *Star Trek: The Next Generation* depicted what turned out to be a highly evolved, godlike species—the "Q"—hauling humankind in the form of the Enterprise crew before a court of law to face the charge that humans are a savage, barbarian race.

Meanwhile, the news media were inundated with reports of sightings of unidentified flying objects (UFOs) and even of aliens kidnapping humans. For example, Whitley Strieber, whom some rank among the world's most famous "abductees,"[7] has offered book-length accounts of his supposedly repeated nocturnal visits as a nine-year-old boy in the summer of 1954 to the Olmos Basin wilderness area near his home in San Antonio, Texas. Here, he claims, alien entities conducted a "secret school" to prepare him and several other children for encounters that would transpire more than three decades later. The aliens conducted painful and humiliating medical procedures on their trainee, Strieber writes, transported him to Mars, allowed him to witness catastrophic events from Earth's past, and showed him his future as well as that of the planet.[8]

Bizarre? Abnormal? By no means! A poll in 1995 indicated that as many as 2 percent of Americans claim to have been abducted by aliens.[9] In 1996, 55 percent of Canadian respondents to a similar poll said that Earth likely had been visited by extraterrestrials, and 43 percent surmised that aliens likely will arrive at some point within their lifetime.[10]

Are these alien visitors friendly? Opinions vary. Some ufologists assert that these supra-human life-forms have come to kick-start an evolutionary spurt that will catapult us into a higher existence. Others suggest they have arrived on the scene just in time to steer us away from the imminent catastrophe that our reckless behavior threatens to unleash on the entire planet.

Others, however, have another, ominous "take" on the situation. For example, Nick Pope, who worked at the "UFO desk" in the British government from 1991 to 1994, is troubled by the implications of UFO phenomena. Based on his analysis of UFO sightings and contact found in the government file, he concluded, "The general memory [of abductees] is that the aliens have no feelings of any kind towards their human captives and regard them rather as we regard laboratory rats." He later offered this warning: "I believe that there is a war going on, a one-sided war so secret we aren't even aware that it is happening. If any of these incidents can be attributed to an alien presence, then that presence is carrying out what can only be described as crimes against humanity."[11]

A Christian Appraisal of UFOs. Are extraterrestrial "visitors" a modern, scientific, and hence more sophisticated way of talking about the beings the biblical writers call "angels"? Are UFOs the vehicles that transport these "angels" from "heaven" to Earth? In the 1970s, Erich von Dänikén offered precisely this conjecture. In his best-selling book *Chariots of the Gods?* he speculated that the ancient stories about the "gods" (or "angels") were the residue of human encounters with visitations from extraterrestrial intelligent life.[12]

There is, however, one debilitating flaw to this theory. Most speculations about UFOs and alien life-forms depict the space visitors as physical beings who, like humans, are the product of the evolution of intelligent life in the universe. The angels of the Bible, in contrast, are not more highly evolved physical beings. Although they may from time to time take on physical form for the purpose of communicating with us, they are actually spiritual beings and their usual habitat is the spiritual, heavenly realm.

Viewed from the biblical perspective, rather than being more highly evolved intelligent life, the angels are in fact "below" humans. Human beings, and not angels, are the crown of God's creative activity. Consequently, one crucial role of angels is to serve God by serving humans. The author of the New Testament book of Hebrews put it this way: "Are not all angels spirits in the divine service, sent to serve for the sake of those who are to inherit salvation?" (Heb. 1:14).

But this raises an important question: What about all the hype about UFOs? Interpreters such as Pope would say, of course, that the explosion of UFO "sightings" ought to awaken us to the grave peril at our doorstep. While his appraisal is debatable, this much seems certain: The current UFO craze is fueled by a growing sense among people today that we have little control over the forces shaping our day-to-day existence. And the inordinate attention devoted to UFOs in turn fuels conspiracy theories and deepens the mistrust of governmental authority. Left unchallenged, such thinking will discourage people from taking ownership of the problems of our planet. And it may eventually even hasten the collapse of our society.

Into this seemingly hopeless and potentially dangerous context of fear of the unknown, the Christian faith brings a message of hope. Whatever may be the truth to rumors of extraterrestrial beings visiting our planet, the gospel declares that the ultimate Power operative in the universe is "friendly," benevolent, and good. Indeed, this Power is characterized by self-giving love (John 3:16). Therefore, regardless of what the future may hold, we need not fear. Armed with faith, hope, and love, we can—we must!—engage ourselves wholeheartedly and confidently in tackling the grave problems we face today (1 Cor. 15:58).

The Souls of Our Dearly—
and Not-So-Dearly—Departed?

A week after moving into an apartment in Brooklyn with her husband and young children, Sophy Burnham supposedly received a mysterious, unexpected visitor—the apparition of a man, who inspected several rooms before finally leaving. Burnham reports that after the ghost's departure, a late-evening telephone call from the landlady provided her with the information she needed to make sense of this unusual experience. Unsure exactly why she had called, the woman proceeded to speak about her late husband's love for the house, especially the rooms now occupied by the renters. The tenant realized that the "ghost" was none other than Dr. Glas. According to Burnham's explanation, he had come to meet the new occupants, and satisfied with what he discovered, the phantom had led his widow to alert her to his identity.[13]

In contrast to theories that speak about visitors from far-off planets, other recent answers to the question "Are we alone in the universe?" look no further than to the terrestrial realm. Angels, they inaccurately conclude, are the spirits of dead humans who for various reasons have not passed over to "the other side."[14]

Popular Understandings of Ghosts. And who exactly are these spirits? Opinions vary.

Some buy into the sentimental idea that angels are the spirits of persons who died while children. This idea was popularized some years ago in the touching Christmas story *The Littlest Angel*, which narrates how a little boy at death became an angel and his most cherished possession, a toy box, became the star of Bethlehem.

Others are convinced that ghosts are persons who suffer untimely deaths, leaving them with unfinished business to attend to. In the late 1980s this theme repeatedly provided the grist for the filmmakers' mill. From *Heart and Souls* and *Field of Dreams* to the cute crimi/love-story *Ghost*, Hollywood played on the sentimentality we feel when we think of dying with dreams yet unfulfilled.

Perhaps the most significant theory, however, is that angels are humans who have attained the goal of their personal evolutionary or spiritual growth. As angels, these deceased people now play some positive role in events on earth.

But what exactly do departed spirits do?

One suggestion is that they provide assistance and comfort to their loved ones who are left behind. Repeatedly today we hear stories about supposed experiences of such help.

Terri Beeler, to cite a typical example, tells of how she lost a lifelong friend, an innocent fatality of a college campus disturbance. Almost immediately after his death she began to sense his protective presence. According to Beeler's report, one week following the funeral, he appeared to her. In her words, "He told me I should not mourn his departure, because he was happy and at peace . . . that we would meet again in his new world and to be patient, that our love would never die." She claims that on two subsequent occasions she experienced "hovering about five feet from the floor" the presence of "a bright mass of energy, a yellow and orange ball about six inches in diameter." In her "conversation" with the apparition she was told that "I was not to fear or worry, because I was being watched over. His protection, caring, and love were continuing, though his physical being was gone." These visitations have had a reassuring effect on Beeler: "Now I accept the fact that I've been blessed to be able to view the dimensions of the other side."[15]

Some people take the idea of gaining assistance from the dead a step further. They look to departed persons for guidance. They are convinced that the dead can serve as "spirit guides" to the living. Whether they be the souls of people known while on earth or the spirits of long-since deceased members of past generations, such spirit guides supposedly inspire us in our pilgrimage, offer wise counsel about what we should do, and even inform us about what we can anticipate in the future.

There is also a dark side to the popular belief in ghosts. Despite the convictions of some that the dead become guardian angels, most people view ghosts in a somewhat ambiguous light. As the chilling ghost stories that fascinated us as children suggest, the fear that phantoms can be malevolent runs deep in the human psyche.

This is evident, for example, in the ancient Greek idea of *daimones*. In popular belief a daimon was "a being, often thought of as the spirit of the dead, endowed with supernatural powers, capricious, and incalculable, present in unusual places at particular times and at work in terrifying events in nature and human life, but placated, controlled or at least held off by magical means."[16] And different societies devise various "magical means" to keep the souls of the not-so-dearly departed at bay.

A Christian Appraisal of the Belief in Ghosts. What should we make of all this? Are ghosts—that is, the spirits of dead humans—in any way connected to the beings the biblical writers call "angels"? Simply stated, the answer is no! The biblical accounts consistently maintain that angels and humans are quite distinct beings.

But we must say more about the belief in ghosts. To persons haunted by the dead, the Christian faith provides helpful news. As we noted in chapter 2, to be human means to be an embodied being. Consequently, we can say categorically that the dead are no longer active on the earth. They have no direct involvement in the realm of the living, whether for good or for ill.

The biblical writers take this matter even further. Repeatedly we read warnings cautioning against being taken in with people who claim an ability to contact the dead. For example, when the ancient Israelites prepared to enter the land of promise, Moses gave them this stern command:

> When you come into the land that the LORD your God is giving you, you must not learn to imitate the abhorrent practices of those nations. No one shall be found among you who makes a son or daughter pass through fire, or who practices divination, or is a soothsayer, or an auger, or a sorcerer, or one who casts spells, or who consults ghosts or spirits, or who seeks oracles from the dead. For whoever does these things is abhorrent to the LORD; it is because of such abhor-

rent practices that the LORD your God is driving them out before you. You must remain completely loyal to the LORD your God (Deut. 18:9–13).

Why did the ancient prophets find such practices so detestable? The obvious reason is simply that the dead are dead. That is, they are no longer active agents in the earthly realm. Nor can they be contacted in any actual sense.

The Old Testament prophets offered another reason as well. Many people consult a medium or soothsayer to obtain guidance, especially guidance about the future. When we look to the dead for answers to life's enigmas, however, we draw our eyes away from the One who alone is both sovereign over the future and the fountain of all wisdom.

Saul's visit to the witch of Endor provides a chilling warning about this. The biblical writer offers this indictment: The king "consulted a medium, seeking guidance, and did not seek guidance from the LORD" (1 Chron. 10:13–14). Several centuries later the prophet Isaiah declared the folly of such actions by posing a rhetorical question: "When someone tells you to consult mediums and spiritists, who whisper and mutter, should not a people inquire of their God? Why consult the dead on behalf of the living?" (Isa. 8:19, NIV).

Isaiah's observation remains appropriate for us today. Why look to our "dearly departed" to provide guidance, comfort, or a sense of well-being? They are dead! Why not look instead to the Living One who alone is greater than death and who cares for us? Why not find the strength and the will to go on in the face of the death of a loved one from the "God of all consolation who consoles us in all our affliction" (2 Cor. 1:3)?

One final question remains. Does this mean that the dead cannot affect our lives? Not exactly. Despite that they are dead, those who have departed this world can exercise great influence over the living. But here's the catch: They are able only insofar as we give them occasion to do so. Whatever power the dead have over the living is derived power. It is a power or influence we the living have endowed them with.

How? In several ways. You endow the dead with power as you choose to be influenced by the stories of encounters other people tell. You empower the dead when you listen to your own inner fears or when you harbor secret wishes for contact with those who have died. But there is an even more sinister potential here. Dark forces also can capitalize on our openness to receiving messages or visitations from the dead.

Heavenly Hosts?

This brings us again to the biblical teaching that our universe *is* populated with other intelligent life. These living creatures are the heavenly hosts, the spiritual beings whom the biblical writers refer to as "angels."

What do the angels do? Should we seek contact with them? Here again confusion abounds. Therefore, we must now zero in more closely on the activities of the angels.

What Do Angels Do?

One day Calvin and Hobbes were sitting on a rock tossing stones into a pond. Calvin mused to his tiger-friend that he was quite sure that angels are everywhere. Noting Hobbes's incredulous response, Calvin explained that he had seen angels on calendars, greeting cards, books—in fact, on most every product imaginable.

Calvin is right. It seems that angels *are* everywhere. What lies behind the upsurge in interest in angels? What ought we to believe about angels?

The Contemporary Interest in Angels

"Meet Your Guardian Angel" screamed the bold-type, enlarged overline to an ad in the March 3, 1996, edition of the *Burnaby Now,* the community newspaper circulated in the Vancouver suburb where I live. The intriguing advertisement continued: "All cultures incorporate the concept of angels. Would you like to meet your own guardian angel? Through progressive relaxation, meditation and visualization, your instructor will assist you in connecting with your own angel. All you need is the willingness to be delighted, an open mind and, especially, an open heart. Sorry, no senior's discount available." The "class" would be held at a local high school. The sponsoring agency? The Adult and Continuing Education division, Burnaby School District 41.

As this "ad" assumes, people today are interested in angels. Why? Many sociologists attribute the preoccupation with angels, as well as the fascination with ghosts, to several aspects of contemporary life: the widespread reaction against the materialism and secularism of Western society; the perceived need for protection in an increasingly unsafe, even threatening society; the desire for certainty and guidance in the midst of the uncertainty of life—and death—today; the desire for meaning in what appears to be the meaninglessness of life.[17]

The sociologists' appraisal confirms what the *Burnaby Now* "ad" presupposed: Many people desire to gain the sense of well-being that belief in angels appears to provide. And they are intrigued at the possibility of actually encountering an angel at some point.

Those who are caught up in the angel phenomenon, however, look in a different direction. They are convinced that the reason for the surge in interest in angels lies with the angels themselves. Angelphiles (lovers of angels), as they sometimes refer to themselves, place their belief in angels within the context of a larger cosmic drama. Humankind is now at a crossroad, they assert. We are facing what may be our final choice, one that will determine the fate of our entire civilization. Angelphiles are convinced that if we ignore what might be the final warning call from heaven, the earth will be engulfed by a reign of evil. But if we choose the heavenly alternative, Archangel Michael will liberate humanity from the influence of the angels of darkness and God's angels will lead us into a higher reality.[18] The angels have stepped up their activity with the goal of influencing us in making the right choice.

Angels and Us

What should we think about all this? Although the Bible is silent about the existence of physical creatures from other planets and warns us about delving in practices related to the dead, the biblical writers readily acknowledge the existence of angels.

Yet, the recent resurgence in interest in angels is not on track at every point. Shouldn't we wonder how it is that contemporary "experts" "know" far more about angels than the biblical writers seem to know? Shouldn't we be concerned that angelphiles elevate angels to a higher plane of importance in the earthly realm than is warranted from the Bible?

The biblical writers present angels in a simple, straightforward manner without the elaborate speculations that so often accompany the pronouncements of today's angel experts. According to the Bible, the heavenly beings exist to praise and serve God (Isa. 6:1–8). As God's servants, they assist in the divine governance of the world (1 Kings 22:19). In this task, they stand ready to be dispatched to protect God's earthly people (2 Kings 6:17) or to carry out divine judgments (e.g., Rev. 9:13–15). As the "cosmic powers" (Gal. 4:3, 9; Col. 2:8, 20), angels seem to promote harmonious social life among humans by working through the structures that make human social interaction possible. The angelic hosts guide these social structures with the goal of fostering true human community.

Angels are interested in the unfolding drama of salvation (1 Peter 1:12). They were active participants in the story of Jesus. They will once again become prominent when Jesus returns (Matt. 13:39; 25:31). The angels worship Jesus Christ, who is their Lord (Heb. 1:5–14). They minister to us at God's bidding (Heb. 1:14), as we noted earlier, but in ways that are largely unknown to us (Heb. 13:2).

Many angel experts encourage people to develop a relationship with angels. The authors of *Ask Your Angels* claim that "we're all capable of walking down a street and having a conversation with our angels. . . . Talking with angels is the most natural thing in the world. . . . When you *Ask Your Angels*, you can be sure that you will be answered."[19] But nowhere in the

Bible are we admonished to seek out angel companionship. On the contrary, our chief concern ought to be to cultivate a friendship with the One who is greater than the angels and whom they themselves serve (Matt. 22:37–38).

Because angels are creatures as we are, to look to them for guidance, whether directly or through practices such as astrology or divination, is senseless. Consider, as an example, an item that has recently made its way onto the shelves of angel boutiques: "Angelic Messenger Cards—A Divination System for Spiritual Self-Discovery." The package boasts, "The angels are teaching us an entirely new and deeply meaningful way to hear their guidance. If you love flowers, you will benefit greatly by working with these Angelic Messenger Cards and real flowers to 'intuit your own personal guidance.' "[20]

Our first response to this piece of blatant consumerism might be to wonder what kind of guidance—beyond one's own "wishful thinking"—a pack of cards and a few flower petals could possibly provide. At best, the "guidance" we discover may be nothing more than the ruminations of our mind.

To leave that matter here, however, would be to fail to see a menacing danger hidden beneath the surface of what might otherwise be dismissed as an innocent diversion. Viewed from the perspective of the Bible, practices that seek advice from other creatures—even heavenly ones—readily become idolatry. Astrology, for example, mistakenly supposes that the heavenly bodies, which are actually only physical creatures, can affect our lives. Consulting a fortune-teller, a diviner, or even an angel assumes that we can somehow gain access to cosmic powers—whether a mortal like Jeane Dixon or the angel Akatriel, revealer of divine mysteries—who know the unknown. In both cases, we are easily led away from the only Source of wisdom. In both cases, we display a lack of trust in God.

One additional thought ought to give us pause. Through practices such as astrology, divination, and seeking to contact angels, we may indeed get in touch with a spiritual force. But we might just discover to our dismay that the force we are dealing with is dark and evil, not good.

The Dark Side of the Heavenly Powers

This brings us to the flip side of the Christian teaching about angels. The biblical writers clearly declare that not all spiritual beings are good. On the contrary, they speak of a "kingdom" of evil personified by the demons and their chief, Satan or the devil.

Satan and the demons are the enemies of humankind. Although they may at times fool people into thinking they are seeking our good (2 Cor. 11:14), their ultimate goal is to prevent us from living according to God's good purposes. To this end, they actively try to thwart the proclamation of the gospel, tempt us to sin, foment persecution against the church, and disrupt the well-being of creation. In their attempt to cause harm, demons endeavor to work through human agents. They purpose to incite people to injure other creatures such as animals, other humans, and even themselves.

The demonic hosts desire as well to bring humans into bondage. They try to enslave individuals through addiction. Their presence can sometimes become so strong that it impairs or distorts their victim's personality. Demonic powers also endeavor to undermine justice and righteousness in human relationships. To this end, they try to coopt social structures.

For example, whereas God intends human government to be a positive force, punishing the wicked and rewarding the good (Rom. 13:1–7), Satan wants to manipulate it for his evil purposes. Even religious structures can come under the influence of evil forces and bring people into bondage to unhealthy legalism (Gal. 3:23–24; Col. 2:20–23) or to erroneous, harmful teachings (1 Tim. 4:1).

Here again, however, the Bible offers what is truly good news. Despite their seemingly awesome power, Satan and the demonic hosts have already been defeated. As we will see in chapter 5, Jesus has won the victory over the powers of evil. Because he is Lord of the cosmos, we need no longer fear the hosts of hell. On the contrary, Christ has punctured Satan's power. Therefore, under the direction of the Holy Spirit we can live confidently in this world and boldly confront the evils that attempt to undermine God's program for us individually, for humankind, and for all creation.

The "Powers" or the Power?

Are we alone in the universe? In a day when the world seems to be in chaos, people are looking for some semblance of stability. For many, the possibility that we are not alone in the universe promises a desired respite. In their desire for the sense of a supernatural presence many people grab the latest pronouncements of angel specialists or look to television programs from the sentimental to the flamboyant in the vain hope that these sources can somehow confirm that we are surrounded by a host of benevolent creatures who are on our side.

The contemporary interest in UFOs, visitations from the dead, and angelic beings, therefore, is not merely a result of human curiosity. On the contrary, it reveals a deeper spiritual quest. At the core of our attraction to the idea that we are not alone in the universe is a sincere desire to find some sort of spiritual dimension to our lives.

While the spiritual quest this cultural phenomenon represents is laudable, it all-too-readily leads people to look in the wrong direction. Indeed, we are not alone in the universe. But our longing to sense that "everything will be all right" cannot be fulfilled by futile efforts at contacting UFOs, receiving messages from "the other side," or even cultivating a relationship with angelic beings.

Whatever powers may be operative in our universe, there is only one ultimate Power under whose authority all lesser powers stand. Whoever else may be "out there," in the end they—like we—are creatures of the one Creator of the heavens and the earth. This loving, powerful Creator alone is the source of solace, hope, and well-being in a world that so often appears to be out of control.

NOTES

1. For lists of the angels, see Gustav Davidson, *A Dictionary of Angels* (New York: Free Press, 1967), appendix.
2. Bernard Ramm, "Angels," in *Basic Christian Doctrines*, ed. Carl F. H. Henry (New York: Holt, Rinehart and Winston, 1962), 65.
3. "Ockham's Razor," in the *Dictionary of Philosophy and Religion*, ed. William L. Reese (Atlantic Highlands, N.J.: Humanities Press, 1980),

399. Erickson offers this definition of the concept: "No more concepts ought to be introduced than are necessary to account for the phenomena." Millard J. Erickson, *Christian Theology,* three volumes (Grand Rapids: Baker, 1983), 1:167.

4. George Gallup, Jr., and Robert Bezilla, "The Good, the Bad and the Ugly: What We Believe about Other-Worldly Beings," *The Vancouver Sun* (December 17, 1994): D10.

5. Nancy Gibbs, "Angels among Us," *Time* 142, no. 27 (December 27, 1993): 56.

6. Marci MacDonald, "The New Spirituality," *Maclean's* 107, no. 41 (October 10, 1994): 47.

7. At least in the opinion of book reviewer John Oliphant. See "War of the Worlds," *The Vancouver Sun* (February 15, 1997): G5.

8. See Whitley Strieber, *The Secret School: Preparation for Contact* (New York: HarperCollins, 1997).

9. Leon Jaroff, "Weird Science," *Time* 145, no. 20 (May 15, 1995): 75.

10. Jim Bronskill, "Canadians Embrace Idea That Earth Not Alone, Poll Reveals," *The Vancouver Sun* (Sept. 10, 1996): C16c.

11. Nick Pope, *Open Skies, Closed Minds* (London: Simon & Schuster, 1996), 24, 220.

12. Erich von Däniken, *Chariots of the Gods? Unsolved Mysteries of the Past,* trans. Michael Heron, Bantam edition (New York: Bantam Books, 1971), 51–52.

13. Sophy Burnham, *A Book of Angels: Reflections on Angels Past and Present and True Stories of How They Touch Our Lives* (New York: Ballantine Books, 1990), 6–11.

14. A 1993 magazine poll suggests that 15 percent of Americans believe that angels are the souls of the dead. "Angel Poll: What Americans Believe," *Time* (Dec. 27, 1993): 56.

15. A letter from Terri L. Beeler to Sophy Burnham as printed in Burnham, *Book of Angels,* 275–6.

16. Werner Foerster, *"Daimon,"* in the *Theological Dictionary of the New Testament,* ed. Gerhard Kittel, trans. Geoffrey W. Bromiley (Grand Rapids: Eerdmans, 1964), 2:9.

17. See the discussion in Ron Rhodes, *Angels among Us* (Eugene, Oreg.: Harvest House, 1994), 33–34.

18. K. Martin-Kuri, *A Message for the Millennium* (New York: Ballantine Books, 1996), 221.

19. Alma Daniel, Timothy Wyllie, Andrew Ramer, *Ask Your Angels* (New York: Ballantine, 1992), 9.

20. Meridith L. Young-Sowers, Angel Messenger Cards (Walpole, N.H.: Stillpoint Publishers, n.d.).

Chapter 4

Which God?

*F*ifty-year-old Rita McClain had begun her spiritual journey in a Pentecostal church in Iowa complete with tent meetings. Unable to cope with the deep sense of personal guilt she believed her church had inculcated in her, she switched to "mainline" Protestantism but then rejected all organized religion at age twenty-seven. For the next eighteen years McClain sought inner peace through rock climbing in the mountains and hiking in the desert. Then an emotionally draining divorce triggered in her a desire to scout her "inner landscape." McClain's renewed spiritual quest brought her first to the Unity church, then to Native American spirituality, followed by Buddhism at a local meditation center.

McClain has melded the diverse strands of her journey into an eclectic personal religion symbolized by an altar in her home, which she continually updates. At present her shrine includes "an angel statue, a small bottle of 'sacred water' blessed at a women's vigil, a crystal ball, a pyramid, a small brass image of Buddha sitting on a brass leaf, a votive candle, a Hebrew prayer, a tiny Native American basket from the 1850s and a picture of her 'most sacred place,' a madrone tree near her home."[1]

McClain's odyssey may be more convoluted than that of most people. Nevertheless, it offers a typical example of the spiritual quest widespread in our society today. Her story likewise indicates that religion and religious practice are alive and well in North America—perhaps to an extent unparalleled in recent history.

And why not? As humans, we quite naturally inquire about our existence. "Who am I and why am I here?" we ask. "Are we alone in the universe?" we wonder. Such questions lead us eventually to inquire about the possibility of Something—or Someone—lying behind it all. We wonder about a "supreme power" over or within the universe. In short, we find ourselves drawn almost inevitably to raise the question about "God."

The Contemporary
Question of "God"

The pastor of a well-established congregation in the heart of Toronto was giving me a tour of the church building and grounds. Gesturing to the regentrification project surrounding the stately structure he remarked offhandedly, "To minister in this neighborhood, we no longer need to *prove* the existence of God. The people here all *assume* the reality of the supernatural."

This marks one of the truly astounding developments in recent years.

Christianity versus Atheism

Throughout much of the twentieth century many people claimed that no supreme power—no supernatural deity—stood behind the world. Rather than being the creation of a purposeful God, they asserted, the universe is the product of blind, random, natural forces.

This position, commonly known as "atheism," was fueled by the modern worldview that demanded rational—even scientific—proof for every assertion. For many, the scientific method simply had no place for any claims about a supposedly supernatural dimension. In the name of rationality and science, therefore, atheists discarded the concept of God.

Christians were quick to respond to the atheist challenge. Christian thinkers sought to engage intellectually with what they saw as the foundational issue of the day, the question of God's existence. In response to the query "Is there a God?"

Christian theologians devised a variety of intellectual arguments to confirm that God exists. They hoped their logical arguments would convince intellectually minded believers of the
cogency of the faith while challenging their atheist opponents
with persuasive rationales for the Christian position.

These arguments took a number of forms. The "ontological"
proof began with a commonly held definition of God and proceeded to show that there must be a Being who corresponds to
the definition. A popular formulation of this proof defined God
as the "most perfect being" and claimed that this God must exist simply because a God who does not exist is not the most perfect being.[2]

Another argument, the "moral" proof, began with our human experience of being moral creatures. C. S. Lewis, for example, argued in his widely read book *Mere Christianity* that
the apparent fact that all human societies acknowledge what
seems to be a universal code of morality indicates the existence
of God as the foundation of our common sense of right and
wrong.[3]

Perhaps the most repeatedly cited arguments sought to
show that the universe has a creator. One variety, the "cosmo-
logical" proof, asserted that because the world could not have
created itself but must have a first cause, God necessarily exists
as that first cause. In the late 1970s the scientist Robert Jastrow
shocked his colleagues by articulating a variation of this proof.
He claimed that evidence points to a God at the foundation of
the cosmic "Big Bang" that launched the universe.[4]

The other argument from creation, known as the "teleologi-
cal" proof, asserted that the apparent design or order in the
universe bears witness to the existence of a cosmic Designer,
just as a humanly devised instrument (such as a watch) suggests the existence of its architect (e.g., the watchmaker). F. R.
Tennant updated the older formulation of this argument so as
to include the theory of evolution. He asserted that the evolution of the universe climaxing in the appearance of humankind
on the earth testifies to the existence of God as the One who directed the entire evolutionary process.[5]

Intellectual arguments such as these became an important part of the efforts by some Christians to convince a scientifically oriented society that belief in God was intellectually credible—even more credible than the atheist alternative. These Christians were convinced that science and faith were not at odds. Instead, in contrast to the claims of atheists, they firmly believed that science actually supported Christianity.

The Conflict of the Gods

Although the challenge of atheism is by no means dead, our situation today is more complex than that of even the previous generation of North Americans. In the past, only two main alternatives loomed in the minds of most people: belief or unbelief—Christianity or atheism. Increasingly, however, we find ourselves living in a world that is no longer the scene of the battle between Christians and atheists. Instead our society has become the focus of a conflict involving many rival deities.

This contemporary "invasion of the gods" includes the phenomenal growth of other world religions on Western soil. The number of North American Hindus, Buddhists, and Muslims has increased dramatically in recent years. Almost overnight it seems, Allah, Krishna, and a pantheon of other deities have taken their place alongside the biblical God in the North American religious constellation.

Long forgotten gods are making their debut as well. Having rejected the God of the Bible, many children of the Enlightenment are discovering pre-Christian beliefs and practices. The religions of ancient peoples are returning in the form of what is called the "new Paganism" or "Wicca." Today nearly every urban area in the United States has a fledgling Pagan community.[6]

Central to Wicca is the belief that the deity is revealed in nature and accessible to everyone.[7] Miriam Starhawk, a self-proclaimed practitioner, reflected this understanding in her illuminating explanation of Wiccan magic: "The primary principle of magic is connection. The universe is a fluid, ever-changing energy pattern, not a collection of fixed and separate things.

What affects one thing affects, in some way, all things: All is woven into the continuous fabric of being. Its warp and weft are energy, which is the essence of magic."[8]

If "connectedness" is the key, why the tie to ancient deities? What importance can paying homage to old pagan gods possibly have? The answer lies in the contemporary appropriation of the work of the psychologist Carl Jung. Jung offered what has become a widely acknowledged explanation of the link between "connection" and the gods of long ago.

Especially important is his idea of the "collective unconscious." Jung theorized that

> [i]n addition to our immediate consciousness, which is of a thoroughly personal nature and which we believe to be the only empirical psyche . . . there exists a second psychic system of a collective, universal, and impersonal nature which is identical in all individuals. This collective unconscious does not develop individually but is inherited. It consists of preexistent forms, the archetypes, which can only become conscious secondarily and which give definite form to certain psychic contents.[9]

The archetypes Jung talked about are actually patterns of instinctual behavior that express themselves in various ways, including dreams and fantasies. But one of the most significant expressions is through mythological symbols, such as the gods. For Jung, the gods represent these human archetypal patterns. Consequently, venerating many gods links devotees to various dimensions of our human existence. Hence, contemporary Pagans conclude that to ignore any particular deity is to ignore an aspect of who we are.

The influence of Jung's theories is not limited to the new Paganism. On the contrary, you can find shades of Jungianism in many places, even in some spiritualities emerging along the edges of Christianity. For example, the proceedings at the highly hailed and hotly assailed Re-Imagining Conference, initially held in Minneapolis in November 1994, included a prayer called *The Blessing over Milk and Honey*. This prayer gives religious expression to certain aspects of women's psyche. Addressing the goddess Wisdom (or the Christian God under the metaphor of Wisdom), the prayer reads, "Our maker Sophia [Wisdom], we are women in your image: With the hot blood of our wombs we give form to new life. . . . Our mother Sophia, we are women in your image: with nectar between our thighs we invite a lover, we birth a child; With our warm body fluids we remind the world of its pleasures and sensations."[10]

The Conflict of the Gods and the Question of God

Followers of the popular comic strip "Doonesbury" will recall that in spring 1997, the baby-boomer Mike, whose first wife had left him for the free-spirited Zeke, married a "Gen X" computer whiz (Kim) of Vietnamese descent. On their honeymoon, the newlyweds visited Kim's home country in part to find her only known relative, a cousin working at a Nike factory. Thinking Kim was a Western social activist, a member of the management team provided her with a personal guided tour of the plant. En route, the guide declared that despite rumors to the contrary a special feeling permeated the Nike factory, namely, the sense among the employees that they were working for something bigger than themselves. Kim's guide cited a large object in the center of the factory grounds as an example of this feeling. He explained that it was a shrine and that every worker was allowed five minutes a day to worship.

Convinced that she already knew the answer, Kim inquired rhetorically whether the object was a statue of Buddha. "Jordan," replied the manager matter-of-factly, referring to the great Chicago basketball player.

As this "Doonesbury" story indicates, religion and worship have become an assumed dimension of the contemporary scene. Religion is alive and well in North America. But many religions now vie for our attention. And each one claims to speak the truth. For many people, therefore, the question is not "Is it proper to worship?" but "To whom will we pay homage?"

This situation is far from new. The first-century Christians, as well as the Hebrews before them, lived at a time when people worshiped a host of gods (1 Cor. 8:5–6). Because each of these gods had a defined sphere of influence, ancient worshipers—like their contemporary successors—did not always pick and choose among them but simply acknowledged all the various deities. Indeed, to neglect any particular god was to reject an area of human experience.[11]

The proliferation of gods in our society, together with the eclectic approach to religion exemplified in Rita McClain's journey, indicates that you and I find ourselves in a context quite similar to the world of the biblical communities. Like they, we live at a time in which many religious ideas compete. In our era of the "conflict of the gods," the same questions arise as were present in the biblical era. We today can no longer simply ask, "Is there a God?" Instead, for an increasing number of people the more important question is "Which god?" or "Whose God?" In short, people today are wondering about the identity of God.

God's Identity

In the midst of the contemporary openness to the supernatural and to spirituality, we find no unanimity about the proper recipient(s) of our religious loyalty. Our society now boasts many conceptions of deity.

It has always been fashionable for Christians to point out rivals to the Christian God and to talk about the deities of contemporary society. But at a time when the main religious options were either the Christian God or atheism, the "gods" that contended with the God of the Bible were understood in a purely figurative sense. The idols that purportedly populated the North American landscape and against which Christian writers railed were "deities" that bore such names as "materialism," "hedonism," "narcissism" and, of course, "scientism."

All that has changed. These more traditional alternative "gods" have not vacated the scene by any means. Yet, as we have noted already, a variety of newcomers have invaded the religious terrain. Like Rita McClain, North Americans construct shrines to a plethora of deities. And these various deities all have names.

How, then, ought we to think and speak about God?

The Demise of the Generic God

In a context similar to our own in which people paid homage to many gods, the biblical prophets adamantly asserted that there is but one God, and this God alone is to be worshiped. The prophets of both the Old and New Testaments were quite clear about the identity of this God. They drew a sharp distinction between the only true God and the deities the nations worshiped. This distinction arose, they declared, because God had revealed the divine name to God's people. Consequently, the prophets identified the only true God by designating this God by name.

Like the biblical writers, we too can no longer speak about "God" simply in generic language. People today don't automatically associate the designation "God" with the God of the Bible. Nor can we naively assume that the various designations we hear today—whether "Allah," "Krishna," or "Sophia"—are simply alternative ways of speaking about the one and only God. The emerging situation in our society in which many gods are vying for allegiance has resulted in the demise of the "generic God."

For this reason, Christians must be specific in designating the God they serve. Only in this manner can we place in sharp relief the distinction between the God of the Bible and the gods that find their way into the eclectic shrines before which people today offer their homage.

The Triune God of the Christian Faith

Who, then, is the God Christians proclaim? At the heart of our faith is the belief that the only true God is the One disclosed in the biblical story as focused on Jesus of Nazareth. The experience of the early Christians with Jesus inaugurated a process leading to the specifically Christian understanding of the nature of God. At the heart of this understanding is the concept of God as the triune One, the three persons (Father, Son, and Holy Spirit) in eternal fellowship.

Why the Christian God Is Triune. The first followers of Jesus inherited from their Old Testament background a strict allegiance to the God of Abraham, Isaac, and Jacob. For Israel, belief in this God precluded the worship of the gods of the surrounding nations (Deut. 6:4–5; 32:36–39; 2 Sam. 7:22; Isa. 45:18). Christians, in turn, claim that the God we worship is none other than the God of Israel, who is the only true God.

The early Christians also confessed that Jesus of Nazareth is the exalted Lord of all creation (e.g., John 1:1; 20:28; Rom. 9:5; Titus 2:13). At the First Ecumenical Council, meeting in Nicea in 325, the church affirmed the belief that Jesus shares fully in the deity of the One whom he called his Father, while being distinct as the Son of the divine Father (e.g., Rom. 15:5–6).

Beginning with Pentecost, Christians also were conscious of the ongoing divine presence within their community. This Reality, they concluded, is neither the Father nor the Son but a third person alongside the other two, the Holy Spirit whom Jesus promised to send among his followers (John 14:15–17). In 381 at the Second Ecumenical Council (Constantinople), the church officially affirmed that the Holy Spirit is fully divine together with the Father and the Son.

In this manner, Christians came to conclude that according to the revelation in Jesus, the only God is Father, Son, and Holy Spirit. This God is one, for the three share the same will, nature, and essence. Christians are not polytheists, for we do not worship three distinct Gods. At the same time, we do not serve some generic "God," but the God who is Father, Son, and Holy Spirit.

What "Triune" Means. Our affirmation of God's three-in-one-ness is not simply a declaration of how we experience God or the way God appears to us. On the contrary, Christians declare that the one God is eternally triune. God is the unity of Father, Son, and Spirit. Not only does each of the three trinitarian persons fulfill a distinctive role in the one divine program for creation, the Father, Son, and Spirit also are eternally distinct from one another, while comprising a unity. In this manner, the one God is a diversity-within-unity or unity-in-diversity.

The understanding of God as triune provides the crucial foundation for the Christian belief that God is characterized by love (1 John 4:8, 16). The Greek word *love* (*agape*) used in the New Testament refers to the giving of oneself for the sake of another. Such active, self-giving love builds the unity within the one God. One way to speak about this great conviction is to declare that through all eternity the Father loves the Son, the Son reciprocates the Father's love, and the love they share is the Holy Spirit. In this way, God is the eternal community of love, and God is love even apart from the universe.

Not only does "love" describe God throughout eternity but it also characterizes God's way of responding to the universe. Indeed, the God who is love naturally acts in love. As the well-known "Sunday school" verse puts it, "For God so loved the world that he gave . . . " (John 3:16). This love, however, is not a soupy sentimentality. Instead it is a "tough love" that seeks to preserve and safeguard the relationship God desires to share with us.

The Christian understanding of God as the fellowship of Father, Son, and Holy Spirit forms a vital foundation for human living. It indicates that the ideal for humankind does not focus on isolated individuals. Nor does God's goal for us lead to the loss of personhood. On the contrary, the God who is triune created us to be persons-in-community.

As a result, reflecting the divine nature requires that we move out of our isolation into relationships with others—relationships characterized by godly love and concern for the other. Hence, trinitarian Christians seek to foster life-in-relationship or life-in-community. It demands as well that we seek to reflect God's loving concern for all creatures by acting justly and serving as instruments in bringing about love, justice, and righteousness.

God and the World

Who is God? Christians respond, God is the triune One, the unity of the three trinitarian persons.

At this point a related question emerges: Who is God in relationship to the world? Once again we find competing ideas present in our society. In this context we must clearly set forth what Christians believe about God.

Our Context:
The New Immanentalism

If you have ever stepped into a Gothic cathedral, such as Notre Dame in Paris, you might still be able to recall the awe-inspiring sense of God's exalted greatness that overwhelmed you when you entered the building. These great churches were the product of the Middle Ages, an era that celebrated the wide chasm separating God from the world.

That is no longer the setting in which we live. Three examples substantiate this point:

After being healed of an acute depression, Agnes Sanford, a charismatic Episcopalian and missionary, devoted herself to healing the mental and physical ills of others. Drawing from the work of Carl Jung, she became a pioneer of what has come to be known as the "inner healing" or "healing of the memories" movement. Sanford once offered this description of the deity she serves: "God is actually *in* the flowers and the growing grass and all the little chirping, singing things. He made everything out of Himself and then He put a part of Himself into everything."[12]

J. D. Salinger's short story *Teddy* features a spiritually sensitive boy who at one point in the narrative reports how watching his little sister drink her milk led him to a great insight: "All of a sudden I saw that she was God and the milk was God. I mean, all she was doing was pouring God into God."[13]

In Alice Walker's novel *The Color Purple*, the delightful character Shug Avery declares: "God is inside you and inside everybody else. You come into the world with God. But only them that search for it inside find it. . . . I believe God is everything."[14]

These examples indicate how different the focus today is when compared to the emphasis of the Middle Ages. Many North Americans now revel in God's presence (that is, God's "immanence") within the universe—so much so, in fact, that the God some people imagine meshes almost completely with the world. We can label this contemporary characterization of God as completely present to, and even subsumed within, the world "immanentalism."

Foundational to this new immanentalism is the belief that all is one. Immanentalists assert that behind (or beyond) our sense that we are separate from one another and from every other entity in the universe is the deeper truth that everything is in fact connected. Any perceived differences between separate entities, whether individual humans, humans and things, or even humans and God, are only apparent.

Some immanentalists are convinced that recent advances in science provide the foundation for their belief about the interconnectedness of the universe. Hence, theoretical physicist David Bohm concluded from quantum physics and relativity theory that the world is an "undivided whole."[15] The contemporary religionist Fritjof Capra built from the work of scientists like Bohm. His conclusion? Because we cannot cut up the universe into "independently existing smallest units" we must see its "basic oneness."[16]

Another scientific discovery, the hologram—a three-dimensional projection produced by the interaction of laser beams in which the entire image can be produced from any one component part—purportedly points in the same direction.[17] For example, George Leonard jumps from this phenomenon to the universe as a whole. He claims that "every piece of the universe . . . contains every other piece."[18] In other words, the universe is a hologram.

If the world is a hologram, not only is God present throughout the universe but in a sense everything is God. (This is known as "pantheism.") And if "God is everything," as Shug

Avery asserts, then it follows that each person—i.e., each human self—is God.

The upshot of the new immanentalism is a deep confidence in our human potential. Perhaps no one was more important in initially popularizing the optimistic message of human potentiality than Napoleon Hill. Hill announced to his readers: "You can do it if you believe you can."[19] To this end, Hill devised what he called the "Positive Mental Attitude Science of Success." Hill's PMA entails "creative thinking," which he illustrates with a discussion he had with a Dr. Elmer Gates. Gates asserted that there are three sources of all ideas: one's personal life experiences, the life experiences of others, and "the great universal storehouse of Infinite Intelligence, wherein is stored all knowledge and all facts, and which may be contacted through the subconscious section of the mind."[20]

Immanentalist spirituality takes all this one step further. Not only can we tap into the divine mind within, we can actually become divine. Rodney R. Romney, one-time senior minister of Seattle's First Baptist Church, announced, "To understand God is finally to realize one's own godhood."[21]

This same idea reverberates through the popular writings of M. Scott Peck. In his widely read book *The Road Less Traveled*, Peck asserted, "No matter how much we may like to pussyfoot around it, all of us who postulate a loving God and really think about it eventually come to a single terrifying idea: God wants us to become Himself (or Herself or Itself)." What does this mean? To Peck the answer is clear: "We are growing toward godhood. God is the goal of evolution. It is God who is the source of the evolutionary force and God who is the destination."[22]

Where did this idea of the fully immanent God come from? Simply stated, the new immanentalism is a repackaging for North American consumption of a basically Eastern idea. In Hindu thought, the *atman* of each person is one with the *atman* everywhere and ultimately with the Brahma, the all-pervasive All, the soul of the universe.

As one of the Hindu sacred texts declares, "Though you do not see Brahman in this body, he is indeed here. That which is the subtle essence—in that have all things their existence. That is the truth. That is the Self. And . . . THAT ART THOU."[23] Maharishi Mahesh Yogi, the founder of transcendental meditation and perhaps the leading bridge for the influx of Eastern ideas into the West, reversed the poignant declaration from the biblical book of Psalms "Be still, and know that I am God" (Ps. 46:10) to read, "Be still and know that you are God."[24] Former Episcopal priest turned Zen Buddhist master Alan Watts offered this similar appraisal: "The appeal of Zen, as of other forms of Eastern philosophy, is that it unveils behind the urgent realm of good and evil a vast region of oneself about which there need be no guilt or recrimination, where at last the self is indistinguishable from God."[25]

What ought we to make of this widely propagated contemporary focus? And what do Christians believe about God's relationship to the world?

God Is Transcendent and Immanent

In contrast to the new immanentalism, the Christian understanding of God seeks a careful balance between two seemingly opposite aspects of God's relationship to the world, namely, between what theologians call God's immanence and God's transcendence. For this reason, our appraisal of immanentalism must begin with a clear acknowledgment that it is helpful to the extent that it reminds us of the great biblical truth, namely, the truth of God's immanence.

The biblical writers speak about a God who is involved with the world God creates, a God who is present to and active within the universe. God's activity includes involvement within the processes of nature. The heavenly Father whom Jesus talked about sends sunshine and rain, feeds the birds, clothes the flowers (Matt. 5:45; 6:25–30; 10:29–30). The God of the Bible sustains life itself (Job 27:3; 33:4; 34:14–15; Ps. 104:29–30). This God is near to each of us as well. To cite the poetic words of the apostle Paul, God "is not far from each one of us. For 'In him we live and move and have our being'" (Acts 17:27–28). And above all, the biblical God is immanent as the one who works within human history.

The contemporary reminder that God is immanent stands as an important corrective to the Aristotelian concept of the divine being so influential in traditional Christian thinking. According to Aristotle, God is the "unmoved mover," the static, unchanging final cause of all motion in the universe. As the final cause, God draws all things (for all things naturally strive toward God). But God remains unmoved by or undrawn to the universe.[26]

The biblical deity, in contrast, is not so far beyond the world that God cannot enter into relationship with creatures. Our God is not a distant deity who can't see and hear, or who can't know what happens to us. Instead, God is present with us and is concerned about us.

While acknowledging that God is actively involved within the universe, Christian belief nevertheless differs radically from certain aspects of the new immanentalism. Christians find the contemporary focus on God's immanence one-sided and out of proper proportion. It must be balanced by an equal emphasis on another dimension of God's relationship to the universe. Starhawk declared unabashedly that if we opened our eyes we could see that "there is nothing to be saved from . . . no God outside the world to be feared and obeyed."[27] Christians, in contrast, find in the biblical narrative a God who *is* outside the world, while actively engaging in the world.

The prophet Isaiah sensed God's exalted status over the world when in his vision in the temple he saw the Lord "sitting on a throne, high and lofty" (Isa. 6:1). No wonder the author of the book of Ecclesiastes cautioned, "God is in heaven, and you upon the earth" (Eccl. 5:2).

Consequently, Christians assert unabashedly that God is not fully immersed in creation. We resolutely refuse to equate God with the interconnectedness of the universe. The biblical God cannot be reduced to the "divine spark within each of us." Nor is God merely the great "Matrix" connecting all living beings.[28]

The word that refers to this other dimension of God's relationship to the world is *transcendence*. Christians declare that God is transcendent, by which we mean that God is distinct from, "above" or "beyond," the universe. Likewise, God is self-sufficient apart from the world. From this vantage point, God freely enters into relationship with the world. Nothing, not even God's own nature, compels God to do so, and although we are created in God's image, God is distinct from the human self.

Rather than being an antiquated trait that must be overcome, as many proponents of the new immanentalism suggest, it is this very distinction between God and the universe that offers us hope. Only a God who comes to us from beyond the world can provide the salvation we need, Christians boldly declare.

God Is Spirit and Person

The careful balance between transcendence and immanence Christians seek to articulate leads us to two related biblical characterizations of God. God's relationship to the universe may be characterized by saying that God is "spirit" and "person."

First, the transcendent, immanent God of the Christian faith relates to the world as "spirit" (John 4:24). To say "God is spirit" means that God is the source of life, the One who creates and sustains life. This God is, of course, the source of human life. In the biblical creation narrative, when God breathed into Adam's nostrils "the breath of life," "the man became a living being" (Gen. 2:7). Indeed, we are all dependent on God for our very lives.

God can be the source of life because throughout all eternity the triune God is the Living One. As the eternal fellowship of Father, Son, and Holy Spirit, God is dynamic, active, and alive. In this sense, God stands apart from the world, while becoming active in the universe as the Life Giver.

Second, the transcendent-immanent God enters into relationship with creation as "person." We can properly speak of God as person because in this relationship God remains mysterious and incomprehensible; we can never understand God completely (Rom. 11:33–34). God is person likewise because in relating to the universe God remains "will"; God has a goal for creation and acts in the world to bring the divine purposes to completion. God is person because in the divine-human relationship God always remains beyond our control. This sets the biblical understanding of God apart from the conceptions of those religious traditions that endeavor to manipulate capricious gods by magic or through some other humanly devised means.

Because we believe God is person, Christians are quick to acknowledge the distinction between the divine and the human. The God who relates to us as Person-to-persons eternally affirms us in our own unique personhood.

This belief clearly sets the Christian understanding apart from the new immanentalism. Whether known as Brahma, the great All, or the life-giving Matrix, the immanentalist God is ultimately impersonal. Viewing God as impersonal eventually leads to a tragic denigration of human personhood. This is evident, for example, in the immanentalist assertion that the ultimate goal of life is to lose our personhood and merge into an all-encompassing Absolute, a point we will explore further in chapter 7.

God Is Good

The Christian understanding of the transcendent-immanent God differs from that of the new immanentalism in another important manner. The two offer opposing understandings about the character of God.

In the perennially popular *Star Wars* epic the inhabitants of the universe know full well that the Force—that impersonal divine reality pervading the *Star Wars* universe—has both a good and a "dark side." For this reason, connection with the force is both exhilarating and dangerous. It can produce both a morally upright hero such as Luke Skywalker and an arch villain of the likes of Darth Vader. In this manner, the George Lucas classic offers a clear expression of a god who is beyond the distinctions "good" and "evil," while encompassing both. This conception of the divine reality resembles the Hindu deity. As the Hindu teacher Swami Vivekananda once asked rhetorically, "Who can say that God does not manifest Himself as Evil as well as Good?"

The biblical God, in contrast, is morally upright, just, and righteous. Goodness is God's actual character. Not only is God morally good, Christians declare that God is also the standard for morality. In fact, God's loving disposition toward creation is the touchstone by which we are to appraise all human conduct.

God, we assert, steadfastly opposes evil, while being compassionate, gracious, and long-suffering with humans (e.g., Ex. 34:6; Neh. 9:17; Ps. 111:4; 116:5; 86:15; 103:8; 145:8; Joel 2:13; Jonah 4:2; Isa. 54:10). The biblical God is "abounding in mercy." No wonder Christians gladly sing the little chorus "God Is So Good," a lyric no self-respecting devotee of Lucas's Force could consciously echo.

Realizing that God is righteous and compassionate leads Christians not only to joyful and awe-filled praise but also to a new way of relating to others. As Christians, we seek to model our lives after the pattern revealed in the biblical story of God. For this reason, John, the "apostle of love," reminded his readers of the connection between God's character and our conduct: "We know love by this, that he [Jesus] laid down his life for us—and we ought to lay down our lives for one another" (1 John 3:16). It is no accident that the Christian faith leads to an ethic of active love for others, an ethic that has no parallel in the other religions of the world.

Half a century ago the Christian writer G. K. Chesterton pointed out how our conception of God sets the Christian way of life apart from the popular contemporary alternative. In his response to the immanentalist concept of the "universal self," he declared, "I want to love my neighbor not because he is I, but precisely because he is not I."[29] Only as we see our neighbor as a distinct person whom God loves and values in herself can we take seriously the biblical command: "Love your neighbor as yourself."

God Is Creator

The God of the Bible differs from the deity of the new immanentalism in one final crucial manner. Christians declare that God is the Creator of the universe. We can bring into sharp focus this Christian assertion by noting how it contrasts with one of the most popular alternatives proposed today, namely, what has come to be known as the "Gaia hypothesis."

The British atmospheric scientist James Lovelock set forth the scientifically unprovable theory, known as the "Gaia hypothesis," that our planet is a living creature. He defined Gaia, named for the Greek goddess of Earth, as "a complex entity involving the Earth's biosphere, atmosphere, oceans, and soil; the totality constituting a feedback or cybernetic system which seeks an optimal physical and chemical environment for life on this planet."[30] He later wrote that at some point in Earth's history, "the living things, the rocks, the air, and the oceans merged to form the new entity, Gaia. Just as when the sperm merges with the egg, new life was conceived." (He is careful to note, however, that he does not mean to imply that the life-form called Gaia is sentient.)[31]

Lovelock takes the hypothesis a step further, however. Rather than being merely a scientific theory, with Lovelock it becomes a religious conviction. He writes,

> What if Mary [the mother of Jesus] is another name for Gaia? Then her capacity for virgin birth is no miracle or partheno-genetic aberration, it is a role of Gaia since life began. Immortals do not need to reproduce an image of themselves; it is enough to renew continuously the life that constitutes them. Any living organism a quarter as old as the Universe itself and still full of vigor is as near immortal as we ever need to know. She is of this Universe and, conceivably, a part of God. On Earth she is the source of life everlasting and is alive now; she gave birth to humankind and we are a part of her.
>
> This is why, for me, Gaia is a religious as well as a scientific concept.[32]

The Bible, in contrast, does not begin with Earth. Instead the Genesis narrative starts with God: "In the beginning . . . God created the heavens and the earth" (Gen. 1:1). According to the Bible, the eternal God is the Creator of the universe. Rather than existing on its own the universe is the creation of God, for God brought the universe into existence.

Further, God created the universe by an act of the divine will. As a result, the universe exists by God's gracious choice. In addition, God created freely. The universe, therefore, does not exist by necessity. Nor did God create by necessity. God was under no compulsion to create.

God's free creation of the world means that God does not need the world to be who God is. Instead, God is completely the loving God apart from the universe. But how is this possible?

The answer to this question returns us to the Christian concept of God as the triune One. As we noted earlier, God is eternally and completely love. One way to speak about the divine dynamic is to say that throughout all eternity the Father loves the Son, the Son reciprocates that love, and the love they share is the Holy Spirit. As the fellowship of the three trinitarian persons, God is fully God—the Loving One—within the eternal, divine life. Hence, God does not need the world to be the God of love.

Why, then, does the universe exist? The only answer can be: Simply because God graciously chooses to create. But why? Once again, only one answer is possible: Because of God's great love.

Here as well the Christian understanding of God assists us. We may speak of the act of creation as the "outflowing" of the eternal love within the heart of God—the love of the Father for the Son, a bond of love who is the Holy Spirit. The Father who loves the Son throughout eternity creates a universe to share in this infinite divine love.

The Father, therefore, is the direct Creator of all that exists (1 Cor. 7:6). But the Christian view of God as the triune One suggests that the Father creates for and through the Son, whom the Bible designates the "Word" or ordering principle of all creation (John 1:3, 14; Col. 1:16a)—the One in connection with whom all things find their meaning (Col. 1:16b). The Father who eternally loves the Son creates the world so that there might be creatures who reciprocate the divine love after the pattern of the Son's love for the Father. The Father creates by the Holy Spirit who is the personal divine power active in the universe, giving it form and birthing its life (Gen. 1:2; Gen. 2:7; 6:3, 17; 7:22; Job 26:13; 33:4; Ps. 104:30).

Christians declare that as Creator, God rightfully enjoys a special status in relationship to the universe. That is, God is sovereign. Sovereignty means that ultimately God alone has the right to declare what creation should be. In stating this, we must keep in mind that the sovereign God is the loving God who seeks only what is best for creation.

In view of the undeniable presence of evil in the world, how can Christians declare that the loving and good God is sovereign? We can find an answer to this weighty question only when we view it from the perspective of the future: One day God will bring all creation into conformity with its glorious design (a theme we will explore in greater depth in chapter 7). In the meantime God is active in our world with this goal in view. And whenever humans acknowledge God, reflect the divine character in their relationships with one another, and obey God's will, the One who will be sovereign becomes sovereign in their lives.

How this is possible leads us to the questions we take up in our next chapters.

NOTES

1. Barbara Kantrowitz and others, "In Search of the Sacred," *Newsweek* 124, no. 22 (28 November 1994): 53.
2. Rene Descartes, *Discourse on Method and the Meditations*, trans. Laurence J. Lafleur, Library of Liberal Arts edition (Indianapolis: Bobbs-Merrill, 1960), 120.
3. C. S. Lewis, *Mere Christianity*, Macmillan Paperbacks edition (New York: Macmillan, 1960), 17–39.
4. Robert Jastrow, *God and the Astronomers* (New York: Norton, 1978).
5. F. R. Tennant, *Philosophical Theology*, two volumes (Cambridge, England: Cambridge University Press, 1928–30), 2:78–104.
6. For information on the origins of neopaganism, see the chapter "Neopaganism" in Wouter J. Hanegraaf, *New Age Religion and Western Culture: Esotericism in the Mirror of Secular Thought* (Leiden, The Netherlands: E. J. Brill, 1996), 77–93.
7. Mia Stansby, "Which Is Witch?" *The Vancouver Sun* (January 22, 1994): B9.
8. Starhawk, *The Spiral Dance: Rebirth of the Ancient Religion of the Great Goddess* (San Francisco: Harper & Row, 1979), 129.

9. Carl Jung, *The Portable Jung,* ed. Joseph Campbell, trans. R. F. C. Hull (New York: Viking, 1971), 60.
10. Jack Kapica, "One Woman's Metaphor, Another Man's Heresy," *Globe and Mail* (March 19, 1994): A1.
11. Robert Packer, "Greek Religion," in *The Oxford Dictionary of the Classical World,* ed. John Boardman, Jasper Griffin, and Oswyn Murray (New York: Oxford University Press, 1986), 254.
12. Agnes Sanford, *The Healing Gifts of the Spirit* (Philadelphia: J. B. Lippincott, 1966), 30.
13. J. D. Salinger, *Nine Stories* (Boston: Little Brown, 1953), 288.
14. Alice Walker, *The Color Purple* (New York: Harcourt Brace Jovanovich, 1982), 166–67.
15. David Bohm, *Wholeness and the Implicate Order* (London: Routledge and Kegan Paul, 1980), 11.
16. Fritjof Capra, *The Turning Point: Science, Society, and the Rising Culture* (New York: Simon & Schuster, 1982), 80–81.
17. George Leonard, *The Silent Pulse* (New York: Bantam, 1981), 68.
18. Leonard, *Silent Pulse,* 69.
19. Napoleon Hill and W. Clement Stone, *Success through a Positive Mental Attitude* ([1960] London: HarperCollins, 1990), 73.
20. Hill and Stone, *Success through a Positive Mental Attitude,* 90.
21. Rodney R. Romney, *Journey to Inner Space: Finding God-in-Us* (Nashville: Abingdon, 1980), 26.
22. M. Scott Peck, *The Road Less Traveled* (New York: Simon & Schuster, 1978), 269–70.
23. *The Upanishads: Breath of the Eternal,* trans. Swami Prabhavananda and Fredrick Manchester (New York: Mentor, 1957), 70.
24. Maharish Mahesh Yogi, *The Meditations of Maharishi Mahesh Yogi* (New York: Bantam Books, 1968), 178.
25. Alan Watts, *This Is IT and Other Essays on Zen and Spiritual Experience* (New York: Pantheon, 1958), 90.
26. Aristotle, *Metaphysics* 1071b–1074.
27. Miriam Starhawk, "Witchcraft and the Religion of the Great Goddess," *Yoga Journal* (May–June, 1986): 59.
28. Rosemary Radford Ruether, *Sexism and God-Talk* (Boston: Beacon, 1983), 258.
29. G. K. Chesterton, *Orthodoxy* ([1908] London: The Bodley Head, 1943), 225.
30. James E. Lovelock, *Gaia: A New Look at Life on Earth* (Oxford: Oxford University Press, 1979), 11.
31. James E. Lovelock, *The Ages of Gaia: A Biography of Our Living Earth* (Oxford: Oxford University Press, 1988), 41, 218.
32. Lovelock, *Ages of Gaia,* 206.

Chapter 5

Who Is Jesus
and What Did He Do?

O ne day Jesus of Nazareth was strolling with his friends
along the dusty roads near the town of Caesarea Philippi. Suddenly he turned to his companions. "Who do people say that I
am?" he inquired. His disciples were stunned. Several opinions
surfaced—John the Baptist come back to life, the long-expected
return of Elijah or a great prophet. Then Jesus focused the question: "But who do you say that I am?" (Mark 8:29).

Jesus may well be the most talked-about person who has
ever lived. And the discussion goes on: among scholars and
theologians, to be sure, but also among people in every corner
of our society. Jesus' name pops up everywhere—in books,
films, TV programs, Broadway shows, even rock music. From
Jesus Christ Superstar to *Godspell*, from *The Greatest Story Ever
Told* to *The Last Temptation of Christ*, from George Harrison's
"My Sweet Lord" to Joan Osborne's "One of Us," our fascination with Jesus repeatedly finds expression.

The man from Nazareth has even accomplished what few
people have been able to pull off: Within a year's time, his "picture" appeared on the front cover of all the major North American newsmagazines, including *US News and World Report,
Time, Newsweek,* and *Life*! Since that breakthrough, he has made
a couple of repeat appearances in *Time*, as well as hitting the
cover of *Atlantic Monthly*.

Despite all the attention, after two millennia Jesus remains as
much of an enigma as he was when he walked this earth—so

much so that a host of writers have found themselves compelled to "set the record straight." From Western converts to Eastern thinkers like Christopher Hills, author of *The Christ Book: What Did He Really Say?*[1] to the flamboyant scholars connected to the "Jesus Seminar" inaugurated in 1985 by New Testament scholar Robert Funk, a parade of people believe they have finally discovered, to cite Funk's words, "the *voice* of Jesus . . . what he really said."[2]

Another author, known under the apparent pseudonym "Levi," goes so far as to claim to have received the "true account" of Jesus' life in a vision, an account that includes details missing from the New Testament, such as Jesus' travels and religious education in Egypt, India, Tibet, and Greece. Levi shared this "revelation" with the world in *The Aquarian Gospel of Jesus the Christ*, a perennial favorite of some since it first appeared in 1908.[3]

But perhaps no one has been more audacious than Norman Mailer. In *The Gospel according to the Son*[4] the novelist offers us a purported first-person memoir written by none other than Jesus himself! For the first time, the man from Nazareth supposedly corrects the exaggerations of his overzealous Evangelists—Matthew, Mark, Luke, and John—who were "seeking to enlarge their fold." Thanks to Mailer, we now have the truth of the matter, at least to the extent that Jesus has been able to remember the key events after all these years. "What is for me to tell," Mailer's Nazarene writes, "remains neither a simple story nor without surprise, but it is true, at least to all that I recall."[5]

No wonder that the cover story of the December 1994 issue of *Life* magazine posed anew the ancient question—"Who was Jesus? Solving the mystery and its significance for today." Although it may not be the first question we raise, "Who was Jesus?" remains the central, crucial question we all must answer. Eventually you and I must come to grips with the identity of this person who our calendars suggest stands at the center of human history.

We now confront the foundational question of our existence head-on: Who is Jesus (and what did he do)?

The Human Jesus

One conclusion finds almost universal agreement today: Whatever else he may have been, Jesus was a human being. Such agreement is right. The Gospel writers clearly portray him as such, and in the fourth century the early church affirmed that Jesus was "truly human."

But what exactly does this declaration mean? And what is its significance?

Jesus the Human

One of my boyhood memories is watching the old adventures of Superman on television. Each program would begin with the thrilling description of our hero's prowess: "Faster than a speeding bullet . . . more powerful than a locomotive . . . leaps tall buildings at a single bound." The reciting of the dictum would build to a climax: "Look up in the sky! It's a bird. It's a plane. It's . . . Superman!"

Each week, as I watched the bumbling antics of the "mild-mannered" newspaper reporter Clark Kent, I knew that beneath the human exterior of this man there was a regal blue uniform bearing a big "S." During each installment I waited with eager anticipation for the glorious moment when the "loser" in the business suit would disappear into a telephone booth, so that our hero could emerge to save the day.

This isn't Jesus.

If the makers of the 1970s box office hit movie *Superman I* were correct, the "man of steel" was no ordinary human being. Instead, his parents had sent him to Earth as an infant just before the demise of their own planet. They had carefully chosen the boy's new home, knowing that it would offer a hospitable climate for him. And before launching the spaceship that would transport him to us, his father diligently distilled all the wisdom and knowledge of his people into a recording that would tutor his little son en route to our world. For his life on earth, Superman would be endowed with every conceivable advantage. Jesus was not.

Unlike the great American hero, the Jesus of the New Testament traveled no shortcut to maturity. He transcended none of the limiting aspects of embodied existence. He was spared no difficulty in making his way in this fallen world. On the contrary, Jesus was subject to the conditions of earthly, human existence, just as you and I are.

As a human, Jesus experienced the range of needs common to us all. These included physical needs—such as the time he arrived tired and thirsty in a village in Samaria after a long journey (John 4:6–7). Jesus also experienced psychological needs, including that of companionship. When filled with despair at the prospect of betrayal and death, for example, he sought out the support of his three closest friends (Matt. 26:36–38). And Jesus experienced spiritual needs—needs that drove him to withdraw from the crowds to seek solitude and communion with the one he called "Father" (Mark 1:35).

Jesus likewise faced times of trial and even temptation. In fact, on three crucial occasions he endured a specially severe testing. All three involved moments of intense (even Satanic) questioning of what he had sensed was obedience to his chosen vocation according to his Father's will (Matt. 4:1–11; 16:22–23; Matt. 26:36–39).

Like you and I, Jesus was limited in many ways. For him, each day contained only twenty-four hours; each week included only seven days. And not only did his life span a finite number of years but it also was cut short by a seemingly untimely death while he was in his prime. Further, during his brief lifetime, Jesus could only be at one place at a time. Nor was he blessed with unbounded energy but needed to "recharge his batteries" just as we do. Jesus was even limited in knowledge (Matt. 24:36). Because he could not do everything, be everywhere, or accomplish everything, Jesus needed to prioritize his life, make choices, and order his activities in accordance with his sense of personal vocation.

Not only was Jesus subject to these common conditions of existence, he developed as a human. Rather than emerging from the womb perfectly mature, he grew physically, intellectually, spiritually, and socially (Luke 2:52). And even in adulthood, Jesus continued to learn through his experiences (Heb. 5:8).

Jesus—The Significant Human

Jesus was a human being. About this there is little disagreement. But what is the significance of his life? Here opinions vary.

Jesus the Teacher. Until recently it was fashionable to emphasize Jesus' similarity to you and me. This fit well with the modern scientific bent toward the "natural" with its attendant skepticism about anything that purports to be "supernatural." As a result, many moderns were hesitant to ascribe any qualities to Jesus that would set him apart from the rest of us. Instead of a supernatural Christ, they were content with a Jesus who is simply quantitatively superior to us, possessing whatever goodness or glory is common—even if only potentially—to us all. "Jesus was a human just like you and I" was the cry of the day. Whatever exalted status the Nazarene deserves, moderns declared, lay in his function of representing, embodying, and passing on to us what we too can become.

But what connection might there be between such a Jesus and us? En route to an answer, many modern people sought to determine what about the Nazarene might transcend his first-century Jewish context. They looked for something in him that is equally applicable in every culture and in every era.

Beginning in the late nineteenth century, the popular "take" on Jesus declared that his timelessness lay above all in his role as a great religious and moral teacher. The famous twentieth-century preacher Harry Emerson Fosdick encapsulated this thinking. In his widely read book *The Man from Nazareth* (1949), he reached the typical conclusion of his day about Jesus' transcultural greatness, a greatness discovered already by his first-century contemporaries:

> Putting ourselves in their places, we may surmise that this
> powerful impression of permanent greatness in Jesus dawned

on them as they confronted the manner of his teaching, and then the substance of his teaching, and then the stature of the personality through whom the teaching came.[6]

In what followed, Fosdick summarily unpacked each of these three aspects of "Jesus the teacher." First, he noted that "Jesus had a way of putting things that time does not wear out."[7] More importantly, he suggested, "Behind the manner of Jesus' teaching was its substance. Grant the transient, contemporary elements that necessarily entered into the Master's message . . . still the profound residue remains—truth applicable always and everywhere to man's deepest moral and spiritual needs."[8] This "truth" included Jesus' message about God's sovereignty and Jesus' insights into human life. Above all, however, Fosdick concluded that "[i]t was the personality . . . through whom the teaching came, who supremely impressed the first disciples, and who still fascinates our imagination and challenges our conscience."[9]

Fosdick's focus on Jesus as teacher did not evaporate with the death of the famous preacher. On the contrary, in the 1990s it reappeared in a somewhat altered form in the work of the highly publicized Jesus Seminar.

Several leading participants in this scholarly circle present the Nazarene as a traveling teacher of unconventional wisdom, a sage in the tradition of the Greek and Roman philosophers known as Cynics. The Cynics were distinctive in appearance, with long hair and beard, ragged clothes, and a walking staff and pouch. Through loud harangues in the marketplace and socially unacceptable behavior, they sought to open the eyes of people to the plight of society and to encourage a life of contented asceticism in accordance with nature.

According to some Jesus Seminar folks, the man from Nazareth fit this mold perfectly. He chose to become a wandering teacher who mocked the pretensions of first-century Jewish society. And he offered an alternative, basically egalitarian social vision.

Despite the scholarly rhetoric lying behind this proposal, it leaves us with the simple question: If Jesus was merely a Cynic sage, how can he have much of anything to say to us today?

This theory is not the only understanding of Jesus that can boast adherents in our society. Others take Fosdick's goal of finding the perennial greatness of "Jesus the teacher" in a somewhat different direction. Their image of the man from Nazareth resembles an Eastern guru or a self-help master. Their Jesus is the great teacher of the way to a higher consciousness, the grand exemplar of what we too can become. Speaking for many proponents of this view, *The Aquarian Gospel of Jesus the Christ* declares, Jesus came to "prove the possibilities of man."[10]

How is this to be understood? Marianne Williamson, a disciple of Helen Schucman who devised the popular *A Course in Miracles,* offered this explanation: "Enlightened beings—Jesus and others—exist in a state that is only potential in the rest of us . . . Jesus and other enlightened masters are our evolutionary elder brothers."[11] And how does Jesus' exalted state affect us? One of Shirley MacLaine's mentors claims to have the answer: The real Jesus "became an adept yogi and mastered complete control over his body and the physical world around him." Having attained this state, he "tried to teach people that they could do the same things too if they got more in touch with their spiritual selves and their own potential power."[12]

While largely propagated in "human potential" and New Age circles, ideas such as these repeatedly find their way into the church as well. For example, Rodney R. Romney suggested that Jesus was "simply a man who knew the laws of God."[13] And this Jesus attempted to impart his perceptive knowledge to others, hoping that through his teaching his followers might "realize the Christ within their own consciousness."[14]

So is that it? Is Jesus simply a human being like you and me, albeit one who attained some higher level or who taught an alternative way of living? How does all this square with the portrait of the man from Nazareth found in the New Testament?

Jesus Our Model. The Jesus of the Gospels claimed to be much more than merely a human among humans. "I am the way and the truth and the life," he boldly announced (John 14:6), thereby asserting that he had come to reveal God's intention for

humankind (Mark 7:9; Matt. 19:1–9). On the basis of this declaration, Jesus enjoined his hearers to follow him, to become his
disciples, to take his "yoke" and learn from him (Matt. 11:29).

Both in his message and in his life Jesus claimed to reveal
God's pattern for human living. Specifically, he announced
and embodied the simple principle that true greatness does not
come through self-centeredness. Nor can we attain first place
through elbowing our way to the front. Instead, greatness in
God's eyes arises through servanthood, suffering, and self-
denial (Mark 8:34–38; 10:35–45). He demonstrated that even
death can be the route to life and blessing to others (John 12:24).
For this reason, the New Testament writers present Jesus as our
example in attitude and conduct. We ought to be characterized
by the same type of humility (Phil. 2:3–8), patient suffering
(1 Peter 2:21–23), and love (Eph. 5:2) we see in his life.

Contrary to what modern people tend to assume, imbued as
they often are with the radical individualism of the myth of the
"self-made man," the model Jesus provided doesn't exalt the
isolated individual. Instead, he indicated that God's intention
for us consists of life-in-community. This includes life in fellowship with the God whom he presented as a loving, heavenly Father, life in fellowship with one another, and life in
fellowship even with all creation.

Hence, the Jesus of the Gospels lived in conscious depen-
dence on the Father and the empowerment of the Holy Spirit.
Rather than being a self-sufficient recluse, he enjoyed the mutuality of friendships. He engaged in compassionate ministry to
the needy, thereby demonstrating that "fellowship" can toler-
ate no limits but encompasses the outcast, the hurting, and
even one's enemies. This Jesus also embraced the wilderness,
enjoyed the beauty of creation, and spoke of a God whose care
extends to the grass and the sparrows. Jesus is not our paradigm
as an isolated individual, but as an individual-in-community.

In keeping with his teaching, the Nazarene ministered to the
disadvantaged and outcasts of his day. So much so, in fact, that
he gained the reputation of being a friend of "sinners" (Matt.
11:19). In contrast to the religious leaders, who placed unbear-

able demands on the people (Luke 11:46), Jesus spoke about a God who was acting on their behalf and who would accept them unconditionally, so long as they came to him in humble faith.

This God, Jesus added, is not impressed by wealth and social standing, nor even by outwardly pious prayers and seemingly religious acts. In fact, the Nazarene pronounced impending judgment on the self-righteous religious leaders and impending ruin on the self-sufficient rich (Luke 12:16–21). He challenged the proud to humble servanthood and called the privileged to lay aside the trappings of social stature so that they might practice true repentance and a changed lifestyle.

Jesus declared that all humans, regardless of social status, share the failure to live in accordance with God's will. He likewise invited all persons to put aside worldly standards of appraisal and see themselves as members together of one humanity standing in need of God's salvation.

As the model human who showed that God's design for us is life-in-relationship, Jesus is the founder of a new humanity, a people-in-relationship. According to the New Testament writers, the Nazarene has overcome old ethnic hostilities and social divisions (Gal. 3:28; Eph. 2:14–15). This Jesus has brought people from every nation into a new company, the church, which the biblical authors designated as his "body" (Col. 1:18).

Jesus' Model and Us

Jesus is the model human. But for whom? The New Testament writers know no boundaries for this claim. In their estimation, his message is for all without regard for human distinctions of sex, ethnicity, or socioeconomic status. But how? In what sense can the life of this one human touch the lives of all—including you and me?

The Maleness of Jesus. One possible answer to this question looks to Jesus' life as a male human being. According to some theologians, Jesus' maleness indicates that maleness itself lies at the heart of what it means to be human and hence that women are in some sense deficient humans. We can reject without too much ado any such suggestion as totally incompatible with the Jesus of the New Testament.

Rather than being the basis for Jesus' significance, in our day the maleness of Jesus is more likely to be a stumbling block: How can the life of a male touch all humans—female as well as male? Indeed, certain contemporary feminists have concluded that Jesus' maleness precludes any attempt to "salvage" Jesus. Mary Daly spoke for many in concluding that a male Jesus is simply "*not* in a position to save us from the horrors of a patriarchal world."[15]

Not everyone, however, has found Daly's radical stance compelling. But wherein lies the way out of this problem? Some propose that we feminize "Jesus Christ" into "Jesa Christa." This suggestion found expression in a feminist crucifix, Edwina Sandys's "Christa," that caused a stir when it was displayed during the Maundy Thursday vigil in the Episcopal Cathedral of New York in 1984. Others attempt to look beyond Jesus' maleness to a deeper humanness he shares with all humans—indeed, almost to the extent that his maleness disappears completely and he becomes a neutered human.

Despite whatever advantages they offer, both of these alternatives suffer from a couple of related difficulties. First, they fail to acknowledge that sexuality—our fundamental maleness and femaleness—is an indispensable dimension of our existence as humans. Second, and as a consequence of the first, these suggestions overlook the reality of Jesus as a particular historical person whose maleness was integral to his life on earth.

The observation that the Nazarene's maleness was indispensable to his ministry points us in the direction of the answer both to our concern about Jesus the male and to our question about his connection with us.

Why was Jesus a male? Jesus' maleness provided the vehicle whereby he could reveal the radical difference between God's ideal and the structures that predominated in first-century society.

Recall that according to the Genesis creation narratives, God created male and female to live in the kind of mutuality that would reflect the image of the triune One. In the Fall, however, mutuality gave way to hierarchy. God described this fallen order to Eve after the disobedience of the first human pair: "Your desire shall be for your husband, and he shall rule over you" (Gen. 3:16).

Into this situation Jesus brought a new paradigm. In both his teaching and his actions, he offered a telling critique of the accepted social order. He reasserted God's original intention for human life-in-community.

Given the context in which he lived, only a male could have offered this kind of radical social critique. As the German Bible scholar Suzanne Heine noted, the Jews of first-century Palestine would have immediately dismissed a female "Jesa" simply on the basis of her sex. Rather than viewing her actions as in any way countercultural, they would have seen her self-sacrificial ministry as merely the living out of her socialized ideal role.[16]

By modeling true maleness in his relationships to women, Jesus declared to all men that the way to life does not lie in acting the part of the strong, dominating, self-sufficient male. On behalf of women, the Nazarene lived as the paradigm human who stood against the male-dominant system that viewed women as second-class persons. Jesus modeled a new order where sex distinctions no longer determine rank and worth. He showed the only possible way for both women and men to leave the past behind, namely, by forgiving and being forgiven, and by seeking together God's new order.

To accomplish this, the male Jesus overstepped the social and religious norms of his day that prescribed the proper manner of treating women. In contrast to both Jews and Romans, he always related to women with the highest respect. Unlike the religious leaders of his day, he taught women as well as men, thereby bringing women into a domain that had been reserved solely for men.

Thus, over the objections of Martha he encouraged Mary, who desired to sit at his feet, thereby calling women away from their servitude role and into the task of nurturing their relationship to God (Luke 10:38–42). In a similar manner, in his response to the woman who blessed his mother for her act in giving him birth, Jesus circumvented the traditional way of affirming women. Instead of mentioning their role in childbearing, he declared that hearing and keeping the word of God is the source of blessing (Luke 11:27).

Jesus' Story—Our Story. This observation leads us to one important way in which Jesus' life becomes a model for all of us— whether we be male or female, whether citizen of first-century Palestine or twenty-first-century North America. The connection arises as we come to see Jesus' story as the paradigm for our stories, as we begin to view his life as the pattern for our own. Jesus' life emerges as our model as you and I become his disciples, as we understand ourselves in accordance with the fundamental pattern that characterized his.

But we must immediately dissuade one another from viewing discipleship solely in the manner popularized in Charles Sheldon's classic novel *In His Steps*.[17] Patterning our lives after Jesus' involves more than simply asking in every situation, "What would Jesus do?" Such an approach limits the scope of discipleship to outward conduct.

Instead, patterning our lives after Jesus means that his life and teaching serve as the standard for us. It means that we evaluate our innermost attitudes as well as our outward actions by comparing them to Jesus. It involves living conscious of our presence before God and continually seeking to follow the life of community with God, others, and creation that characterized Jesus. It means as well that we become conscious of how we fail to measure up to the standard of his life and teachings, and that we come in humble repentance and faith to the faithful, forgiving God about whom Jesus spoke and to whom he pointed.

Jesus' story becomes ours as we derive our identity from his. When our encounter with the story of Jesus calls into question our former attempts to make sense out of our lives, that is, when it has destroyed our old identity, Jesus' model life offers us a new paradigm. His story gives us a new set of categories through which we can draw the variegated strands of our lives into a single whole.

Above all, the paradigmatic life of Jesus lifts us out of our isolation into the life-in-community—the life of fellowship with God, one another, and all creation—he pioneered. As we will see more clearly in chapter 6, the quest for life-in-community draws us into fellowship within the community of his disciples.

This leads us again to the maleness of the human Jesus. Whether male or female, each of us can find true identity only through life-in-community. Because this divine pathway to life is often more readily understood by women, Jesus' maleness stands as a special reminder to men that they must follow the same path, if as males they would discover the nature of their fundamental humanness according to God's design.

Jesus—Our Pattern. Jesus the human has revealed what true humanness as intended by God is. In the man from Nazareth we find the kind of life God desires for us all. But we have not yet mentioned what for the New Testament is the most important dimension of Jesus' role as our pattern.

According to the biblical writers, the ultimate focal point of God's design for humans does not lie in the life of the earthly man but in the risen Jesus. The early believers asserted that in raising the crucified one from the dead, God transformed Jesus' earthly, bodily existence into a glorious, incorruptible reality. And this transformed humanness is precisely God's design for us!

To cite the words of Paul's intriguing comparison between Adam and the risen Jesus: "Just as we have borne the likeness of the earthly man, so shall we bear the likeness of the man from heaven" (1 Cor. 15:49). How does this happen? Paul then explains that we will undergo a glorious transformation when Jesus returns: "For the trumpet will sound, the dead will be raised imperishable, and we will be changed" (v. 52). Through this transformation, we will come to reflect the resurrected Jesus. Simply stated, "We will be like him" (1 John 3:2).

In short, then, only the risen Jesus shows us the true humanness God intends for us. Looking to the risen Jesus allows us to see how God's purposes stand in stark contrast to our present human experience. God has created us not for estrangement but for fellowship, not for death but for life, not for bondage but for freedom.

But introducing the resurrection has led us beyond the realm of the merely human. It raises the question, Is Jesus more than human? Is Jesus the Christ? Is Jesus divine?

More Than a Man?

Most people readily acknowledge that some two thousand years ago a man named Jesus walked the roads of Palestine. Many also admit that there was something special about him. Yet the question remains, Is Jesus more than a mere human?

Jesus' early disciples became convinced that there is indeed "more." They concluded that he revealed not only the divine pattern for human living but the very heart of God as well. As in Peter's response to Jesus' query at Caesarea Philippi, they came to acknowledge that the Nazarene is none other than the Christ (Mark 8:29). They concluded that he was the long-expected one sent by God. In fact, he was nothing less than "God with us" (Matt. 1:23).

What led them to this conclusion? And what does all this mean for us today?

Jesus and the Resurrection

In his widely read book *Basic Christianity*,[18] John Stott concluded that the Jesus of the Gospels made a seemingly audacious claim about his own identity. He announced that he is the divine Son of the eternal Father. Stott saw this bold assertion present in four aspects of Jesus' life.

First, while demanding humility in others, the Nazarene repeatedly pointed to himself, allocating such accolades as the "bread of life," the "light of the world," the "resurrection and the life," the fulfillment of the Old Testament, and the One who would draw all persons to himself. Second, according to Stott, the signs Jesus performed, such as changing water into wine, feeding the multitudes, restoring sight to the blind, and raising the dead, were implicit announcements that he was inaugurating God's new order. Third, by speaking of himself as the one who forgives sins, bestows life, teaches truth, and even judges the world, Jesus exercised divine prerogatives and thereby linked himself closely with God. But above all, Stott's Jesus offered an explicit declaration of his identity when he claimed a unique relationship with the Father (John 10:30–33), appropriated to himself the divine "I Am" name (John 8:51–59), and accepted the worship of his disciples (John 20:26–29).

What can we conclude from this? In the modern era, many biblical scholars discounted most aspects of the portrait of the Nazarene the four Gospels present. Rather than the authentic claims of Jesus himself, scholars announced, such lofty assertions as those Stott compiled are simply the later embellishments produced by the early believers.

Today, however—in the wake of Jim Jones, David Koresh, Luc Joret, and Sun Myung Moon—the idea of a human being making lofty claims no longer seems so far-fetched.

At 1 p.m. on June 25, 1997, nine-year-old Lo Chi-Jen arrived at the Vancouver, B.C., airport aboard Air Canada flight 533 from Los Angeles. Some eighteen months earlier, the boy had heard the voice of God revealing to him his true identity. Since then, members of the God's Salvation Church have acclaimed him the "Jesus of the East." With his entourage, Lo Chi-Jen came to Vancouver hoping to meet the Jesus of the West, who supposedly was born in the Canadian city in 1969.

At the airport, a thirty-four-year-old man who went by the name David approached Lo Chi-Jen. David explained how he had hitchhiked to the city after receiving a vision. "I was called," the man announced. "I have gone through an awakening." But Hong-Ming Chen, abbot of the church, wasn't convinced. "You are not the one," he informed a disappointed would-be messiah.[19] The Jesus of the West did not show up.

As this incident vividly reminds us, Jesus of Nazareth is not the only person in history who has claimed a unique relationship with God. Yet we find something noteworthy here. Jesus looked for—even demanded—a future vindication of his claim. He boldly asserted that his heavenly Father would one day exonerate him and his ministry.

According to the New Testament writers, God did just that. The Father decisively confirmed the claim of the Son. How? God raised the crucified Jesus from the dead.

For modern people, of course, the possibility of an actual resurrection is out of the question. The dead simply do not rise. Therefore, any suggestion that Jesus came back to life, and hence that this was God's confirmation of his person and ministry, cannot be seriously entertained. Hence, modern critics dismiss the traditional Christian assertion that Jesus is the Christ. "Whoever he may have been, Jesus was not God," they summarily declare. For the modern thinker, this can be the only credible conclusion about the matter.

Nevertheless, something did happen between Good Friday and Easter Sunday. The biblical writers point out that the tomb where Jesus' body had been placed was empty. They report that on several occasions the risen Jesus appeared to gathered groups of his disciples. Although skeptics have offered supposedly naturalistic explanations for these occurrences or alternative interpretations of the data, none has provided a completely satisfying, unassailably cogent replacement for the conclusion that Jesus had indeed come forth from the dead.

In addition, the phenomenal growth of the early church and the change in the day of worship among the disciples of Jesus—from Saturday, in accordance with the Old Testament law, to Sunday, in honor of the day of resurrection (e.g., 1 Cor. 16:1–2; Rev. 1:10)—offer corroborative support for the resurrection conclusion.

Indeed, *something* happened. But what is the significance of this purported event?

Evolutionary Trailblazer
or Revelation of God?

When coupled with Jesus' own claim about his identity, the resurrection provides a powerful foundation for the Christian belief that the Nazarene is the Christ, the divine Son, the One sent by God with a special mission. Today, however, the question is not so much, Is Jesus the Christ? or even, Is Jesus divine? Instead, the issue is Jesus' uniqueness: Is Jesus alone the Christ? Is he uniquely divine?

The Exemplar of "Christ Consciousness." Many people in our society readily acknowledge that something happened to Jesus in the intriguing hours between his death on the cross and Resurrection Sunday. And they might quickly add that he is the "Christ." But in what sense are we to understand this?

For some people the lofty declarations "Jesus is risen" and "Jesus is the Christ" suggest merely that at the end of his earthly life Jesus entered a higher state of consciousness. His "resurrection" means that Jesus passed over into another realm. His "deity" refers to his ranking among a select group of the spiritually enlightened. In short, Jesus became one of our "evolutionary elder brothers," to cite again Marianne Williamson's phrase.

If Julia, the leading female character in John Redfield's runaway bestseller *The Celestine Prophecy* and mouthpiece for the author, is correct, such a "cross over" to the higher realm occurs sporadically. Every now and then, a person attains the kind of spiritual insight that allows her to vibrate at a sufficiently high frequency so as to fade from view here. In fact, each of us has the potential to do so. Consequently, Julia is hopeful that "our increased perception and vibration will open us up to a Heaven that is already before us" but which we simply cannot see as yet.[20]

Obviously, to proponents of this viewpoint Jesus' "resurrection" and attainment to "deity" is not an uncommon phenomenon. Nor should we limit the title "Christ" to the Nazarene. Instead, in some sense it designates every human, at least potentially. Marianne Williamson offered this illuminating explication: "The word Christ is a psychological term. No religion has a monopoly on the truth. Christ refers to the common thread of divine love that is the core and essence of every human mind."[21] In a similar manner David Spangler explained, "The energy that is the Christ is that life, love, intelligence, energetic power which maintains all creation in existence. It is within each one of us."[22]

If "Christ" is (potentially) present in us all, Jesus is not the Christ per se. Rather, "Christ" is a status he attained. More specifically, it is a state of consciousness Jesus discovered within himself. So why is this Jesus important? Proponents theorize that above all he is an exemplar of what many call the "Christ consciousness" available to all humans. As with other spiritual giants, Jesus' attainment of enlightenment stands as a model to you and me, they claim. Following his lead, advocates add, our goal ought to be to gain the same "Christ consciousness" he knew and thereby to join Jesus in the realm beyond.

What exactly is this exalted state? According to David Spangler, what Jesus discovered was simply his connection with the universe, and thus his connection with God. Spangler's Jesus came to realize, "I am one with the whole, one with God."[23] The Jesus of *The Aquarian Gospel* offered a similar declaration: "The universal God is one, yet, he is more than one; all things are God; all things are one."[24] All this is reminiscent of the early noncanonical Gospel of Thomas, which reported Jesus as saying, "It is I who am the light which is above them all. It is I who am the all. From me did the all come forth, and unto me did the all extend. Split a piece of wood, and I am there. Lift up the stone, and you will find me there."[25]

In short, the "Christ consciousness" certain contemporary writers talk about is nothing else than the realization of the interconnectedness of the universe. This observation returns us to the immanentalist understanding of God we noted in chapter 4. The Jesus of the new immanentalists is merely the embodiment and herald of the all-inclusive All. As our evolutionary elder brother, he points the way and bids us follow. He urges us to discover within ourselves the perennial truth of cosmic unity he discerned two millennia ago.

Is this the Jesus of the New Testament and of the Christian faith? Hardly.

Jesus the Revealer of God. One of the great religions of the world is Hinduism. This venerable religious tradition teaches that the divine reality can be represented in innumerable forms, each symbolizing something about the divine while not exhausting its fullness. Of these forms, the most helpful are the various divine manifestations as human beings. According to Hinduism, Jesus is one such manifestation, but so are Rama, Krishna, Buddha, and many others. In the end, then, all religious leaders point to one truth, and all religions eventually lead to the same truth. As the nineteenth-century Hindu saint Ramakrishna declared,

> God has made different religions to suit different aspirants, times, and countries. All doctrines are only so many paths; but a path is by no means God Himself. Indeed, one can reach God if one follows any of the paths with whole hearted devotion. One may eat a cake with icing either straight or sidewise. It will taste sweet either way.[26]

For this reason, a Hindu can declare, "Krishna is lord" and "Jesus is lord," simultaneously without contradiction.

A Christian cannot.

The early believers were not merely convinced that Jesus was a human being who showed us how to live, that is, who embodied God's intention for us as humans. The resurrection of the crucified Jesus also brought them to conclude that Jesus is who he claimed to be—the divine Son of the eternal Father. Jesus, therefore, is the revelation of God, they concluded.

Like the early believers, in the Nazarene we too find clearly pictured what God is like. In Jesus, we see God!

Christians declare that Jesus is the one in whom we find the fullest understanding of who God is and of what God is like. He is the bearer of the most complete vision of the nature of God. What is this vision? Above all, Jesus spoke about the God who is love. His life illustrated the qualities of that divine love. For example, the loving God seeks the lost, suffers with the afflicted, and redeems the fallen. This God is likewise lovingly jealous. That is, God seeks to preserve the love relationship with creation and therefore acts as the righteous judge.

But the picture of God we find in Jesus goes deeper. To pick up the theme we developed in chapter 4, the loving God whom Jesus reveals is triune. Insofar as Jesus reveals the triune God, he alone is the Christ. Only Jesus is the divine one, "God with us."

However, let's not misunderstand the implications of this

bold assertion. We are not claiming that there can be no knowledge of God apart from Jesus. We are not precluding the possibility that many truths about God can be found in other religious traditions. On the contrary, wherever people are drawn to worship the One whom they perceive to be the Most High, they are acknowledging the only true God, the one who is revealed through Jesus Christ. What we're saying, then, is this: The God whom the nations seek and whom they worship under various guises Jesus has disclosed. And this Most High God is none other than Father, Son, and Holy Spirit.

But we must take this a step further. Because he has brought this more complete picture of God, Jesus mediates to us a fuller relationship with God. Through Jesus, rather than groping after the divine reality through the multiplicity of symbols present among the various religions, we know God in God's triune personhood. By the power of the Holy Spirit—who is the Spirit of the relationship between the Father and the Son—we share in the fellowship the Son enjoys with the Father. Thereby, we enter into a fuller community with God than is enjoyed in any other religious tradition.

Herein, then, lies Jesus' uniqueness. Whereas various religious leaders have offered spiritual insights, no one parallels Jesus, for his surpassing greatness moves beyond his teaching; it encompasses his person (which his teaching, in fact, served to underscore). By pointing to the one whom he called his heavenly Father, by announcing that he was the Son of the eternal Father, and by promising that he would send the Holy Spirit, Jesus laid the foundation for a new understanding of the divine reality, at the heart of which he himself stands. Indeed, so central is Jesus to the understanding of God he revealed that to reduce him to the level of other great teachers is tantamount to destroying the very concept of God he mediated to us and hence the very identity he claimed for himself.

The writer of the Fourth Gospel culminates the prologue to his portrait of Jesus with this ringing affirmation: "The Word became flesh and lived among us, and we have seen his glory, the glory as of a father's only son, full of grace and truth" (John

1:14). In Jesus, the early witnesses saw the divine glory. They were convinced that Jesus' brief historical life was more than a blip in time. Instead, he had disclosed the very heart of eternity. Hence, Paul declared about the Nazarene, "For in him all the fullness of God was pleased to dwell" (Col. 1:19). In short, the early church concluded that Jesus is the "incarnation" of God. We can affirm no less.

How Does Jesus Affect Us?

Our discussion thus far has implicitly indicated that Jesus' identity is closely intertwined with what he did. By his teaching and actions, he demonstrated the loving heart of God. In so doing, he revealed that the one God is the fellowship of Father, Son, and Holy Spirit. But it remains for us to explore how exactly Jesus' life affects you and me today.

Exemplar of "Christ Consciousness" or Crucified Savior?

"At this moment of our planetary birth," Barbara Marx Hubbard announced, "each person is called upon to recognize that the 'Messiah is within.' Christ consciousness or cosmic consciousness is awakening in millions of Christians and non-Christians."[27] Hubbard is convinced that this "messiah within" will lead us into a glorious future.

The esoteric Jesus of the Gospel of Thomas issued this invitation: "He who will drink from my mouth will become like me. I myself shall become he."[28]

Agnes Sanford, the charismatic Episcopalian missionary who later devoted herself to healing the mental and physical ills of others, declared that Jesus Christ "became forever a part of the mass mind of the race . . . a part of His consciousness is forever bound up with the deep mind of man."[29] Through his incarnation, Christ entered "into the collective unconscious of the race, into the deep mind of every person, there being available for healing and for help."[30]

As these statements indicate, for the connection between Jesus of Nazareth and us, the new immanentalists look to the "Christ consciousness" we all share.

In his book *Philosophical Fragments* (1844),[31] the nineteenth-century Christian philosopher Søren Kierkegaard outlined two types of religion. The first asserts that truth is present within each human being. If truth is already latent with us, what we need for this truth to emerge is a "midwife," someone who assists us in giving birth to that truth. This "midwife," of course, is incidental to the process—anyone could fulfill this role, at least theoretically. And in the end, knowledge of God comes about as we come to know ourselves, for in so doing we discover the truth present within.

The second type of religion Kierkegaard described is categorically different from the first. It asserts that we are in fact destitute of truth. What we need to gain truth is a teacher, someone who brings us the truth and who likewise provides us the means for understanding the truth. Such a teacher, Kierkegaard added, is not merely a midwife. Instead, this teacher is "Savior" and "Redeemer."

Kierkegaard labeled the first type "the religion of immanence." The second, in contrast, is "the religion of otherness." Or, to attach the name of a historical figure to each, the first is the religion of Socrates; the second, the religion of Jesus. According to Kierkegaard, the teacher who brings truth is the Christ.

Kierkegaard's portrayal takes us back to the New Testament, more specifically, to the center of the gospel story—the death and resurrection of Jesus of Nazareth—and to Jesus' mission as our Savior.

Jesus—The Man Sent to Die

The Jesus of the Gospels knew he had come for a purpose. His special mission in the divine program entailed fulfilling a role the prophet Isaiah had described in detail centuries earlier, that of being God's Suffering Servant (Isa. 42:1–4; 49:1–6;

50:4–11; 52:13–53:12). This purpose meant that like the ancient prophets, he too would die. Indeed, he declared that he would willingly give his life (John 10:11, 18), for dying marked the high point of his obedience to the will of his Father (John 12:28).

Viewed from the perspective of the resurrection, the cross marks the climactic moment of Jesus' entire life. His death gloriously displayed what he had proclaimed in his teaching and modeled in his life: that losing one's life is the means to finding life. Jesus' death, therefore, is the revelation of true life—life-in-community.

Jesus, however, intended more than this. His death not only would illustrate the way to true living but also would actually make life available to his followers. During his final supper with the disciples, Jesus illustrated the point by offering them bread, symbolizing the giving of his life in death for them, and wine, representing the pouring out of his blood so that they might participate with him in God's coming reign.

But perhaps this was all merely a pipe dream. Jesus' life ended in tragedy—he was crucified as a common criminal. Perhaps the cross calls into question Jesus' entire vision. Maybe his life—and therefore our lives—was ultimately meaningless.

According to the writers of the New Testament, Good Friday did not spell the end of his story. Rather, it gave way to Resurrection Sunday. This event, Jesus' resurrection, dispels the darkness of the cross. When seen through the eyes of Easter, the crucifixion is not the tragic end to the life of a miracle worker who met with stiff opposition. Rather, it is the glorious climax to the self-giving obedience of the one who saw himself as the man born to die. Hence, only in the light of the resurrection does Jesus' death make sense.

But the question still remains: How does this affect us?

Jesus' Death on Our Behalf

In chapter 3 we indicated how humans—you and I—have become God's enemies. We sense a deep alienation—from God, from one another, from all creation, and even from ourselves.

Yet God did not create us for estrangement but for fellowship, not for death but for life, not for bondage but for freedom. The New Testament writers declare that this has been accomplished through Jesus' death and subsequent resurrection. More specifically, Jesus opened the way to life, thereby accomplishing for us what we are helpless to do for ourselves. Through this self-giving act Jesus overcame our failure—our sin, to use the central biblical word—and everything that prevents our participation in God's purpose for our existence.

How? To answer this question, the New Testament offers several interconnected pictures of Jesus' death on our behalf. First, the biblical writers declare that Jesus' death is a sacrifice that "covers" our sin. Jesus bore our guilt so that the wall that bars us from God's presence can be torn down.

Second, Jesus dethroned every alien power—including every addiction—that would hold us in bondage, entrap us, and destroy our lives (e.g., Col. 2:15). Stripped of their power, these forces need no longer bind us. They cannot separate us from God and God's love (Rom. 8:38–39), nor prevent us from returning to our heavenly Father.

The most tenacious of these is the sinister power of death (Rom. 8:2). The good news of our faith is that Jesus tasted death for us. Jesus went through death. But because God did not abandon Jesus, his death was overcome in resurrection. Jesus' death and resurrection are God's promise that death need not have the last word for us either. One day we too can join Jesus in the resurrection.

In the meantime we still die, of course. But by going through death on our behalf, Jesus has transformed the experience for us. Because of his death, we no longer need to die alone. Nor do we need to die into isolation. Instead we die as those surrounded by the love of the Father of Jesus. For us, therefore, death has lost its terror.

Perhaps most significant, however, is a third picture. Through his death Jesus bore the cost of transforming us from God's enemies into God's friends.

As you yourself have no doubt experienced, a cessation of

hostilities never comes without costs. Suppose someone dear to you has wronged you. Suppose as well that after some reflection you realize that the broken relationship will be restored only if you make the first move. Doing so, however, means that even though you are the innocent person you must take on yourself the evil of the severed relationship. You bear not only the pain of your own hurt but the enmity of the other as well. In taking the first step you assume the place of the guilty party; you carry the shame of the offending act.

In Christ, God did just that. God took the initiative to bring an end to our enmity and hostility so that fellowship may be restored. In Jesus, God willingly bore the pain and the hurt caused by our failure.

How? The Gospel writers report that on the cross Jesus was forsaken by God. Through his experience of God-forsakenness Jesus bore our alienation. But not only did Jesus endure the breach of community with his Father, the Father experienced the breaking of fellowship with the Son. The consequences of our hostility toward God interrupted the relationship between Jesus and his Father. The cross, therefore, marked the entrance of the pain of our human failure into the very heart of God, so that we might share in the eternal fellowship between the Father and the Son.

By taking the pain of our failure into his relationship with the Father, Jesus inaugurated a new fellowship of humans—his "body," the church. As the fellowship of Jesus' disciples, we experience a foretaste of the eternal community for which God created us and which we will enjoy fully when Jesus returns in glory. Until that day, the risen Jesus remains with us, for he is present among us through his Spirit.

Jesus—Our Hope

If left to our own devices, we are destitute and devoid of hope. We do not have the resources within ourselves to overcome our hapless, deplorable plight. But Jesus—"God with us"—has come! Through his life, death, and resurrection, he not only has provided a model for living but has rescued us from our failure. Through the provision of his Spirit, he offers the resources needed for us to begin to live in accordance with God's design.

No wonder the biblical writer spoke of Jesus as "the author and perfecter of our faith" (Heb. 12:2). No wonder the nineteenth-century hymn writer declared, "My hope is built on nothing less than Jesus' blood and righteousness."[32]

NOTES

1. Christopher Hills, *The Christ Book: What Did He Really Say?* (Boulder Creek, Calif.: University of the Trees Press, 1980).
2. Robert W. Funk, "The Issue of Jesus," *Foundations and Facets Forum* 1, no. 1 (1985): 7.
3. Levi [H. Dowling], *The Aquarian Gospel of Jesus the Christ* ([1908] London: L. N. Fowler, 1947).
4. Norman Mailer, *The Gospel according to the Son* (New York: Random House, 1997).
5. Mailer, *Gospel according to the Son*, 4.
6. Harry Emerson Fosdick, *The Man from Nazareth* (New York: Harper and Brothers, 1949), 242.
7. Fosdick, *Man from Nazareth*, 242.
8. Fosdick, *Man from Nazareth*, 243.
9. Fosdick, *Man from Nazareth*, 246.
10. Levi, *Aquarian Gospel*, 255 (chap. 179, v. 45).
11. Marianne Williamson, *A Return to Love: Reflections on the Principles of "A Course in Miracles"* (New York: HarperCollins, 1992), 38.
12. MacLaine, *Out on a Limb*, 236.
13. Romney, *Journey to Inner Space*, 28.
14. Romney, *Journey to Inner Space*, 29.
15. Mary Daly, *Beyond God the Father: Toward a Philosophy of Women's Liberation* (Boston: Beacon, 1973), 96.
16. Suzanne Heine, *Matriarchs, Goddesses and Images of God*, trans. John Bowden (Minneapolis: Augsburg, 1989), 137–45.
17. Charles Sheldon, *In His Steps* ([1896] Nashville: Broadman and Holman, 1995).
18. John R. W. Stott, *Basic Christianity*, second edition (London: InterVarsity, 1971), 21–34.
19. Ian Mulgrew, "Jeans-Clad 'Jesus of the East' Waits in Vain at Airport for Reunion with 'Jesus of the West,'" *The Vancouver Sun* (June 26, 1997): B1.

20. James Redfield, *The Celestine Prophecy: An Adventure* (New York: Warner Books, 1993), 242–43.
21. Williamson, *Return to Love,* 29.
22. David Spangler, *Reflections on the Christ* (Forres, Scotland: Findhorn, 1978), 14.
23. Spangler, *Reflections on the Christ,* 16.
24. Levi, *Aquarian Gospel of Jesus the Christ,* 56 (chap. 28, v.4).
25. "The Gospel of Thomas," trans. Thomas O. Lambdin, in *The Nag Hammadi Library in English,* ed. James M. Robinson, third edition (San Francisco: Harper and Row, 1988), 135.
26. *The Sayings of Sri Ramakrishna,* ed. Swami Abhedananda (New York: The Vedanta Society, 1903), as quoted in Huston Smith, *The Religions of Man,* Perennial Library edition (New York: Harper and Row, 1958), 86.
27. Barbara Marx Hubbard, *The Evolutionary Journey* (San Francisco: Evolutionary Press, 1982), 157.
28. "Gospel of Thomas," 137.
29. Agnes Sanford, *The Healing Gifts of the Spirit* (Philadelphia: J. P. Lippincott, 1966), 136.
30. Sanford, *Healing Gifts of the Spirit,* 116.
31. Søren Kierkegaard, *Philosophical Fragments,* trans. David F. Swenson, revised Howard V. Hong (Princeton: Princeton University Press, 1962), 11–27.
32. Edward Mote, "The Solid Rock."

Chapter 6

What Am I Searching for . . . and How Do I Find It?

*I*n her big hit "All I Really Want" (1996) pop singer Alanis Morissette sifts through the competing desires she finds present within and around her. In the lyrics of the rackety song, she rambles through a hodgepodge of seemingly disconnected preferences. Yet couched within it all lies something deeper. As Morissette lives in an unjust world populated by picky people, what she really wants is patience and peace. Feeling herself knocked down and strung out, she longs for deliverance and some means "to calm the angry voice." Alone and frustrated by the apathy and superficiality of others, she desperately yearns for a soul mate, a kindred spirit, someone who truly understands.

Monopolizing the airwaves about the same time as Morissette's song was Joan Osborne's "One of Us." One poignant line pictures humans as lost passengers on a bus headed nowhere. The lyrics muse whether God might be a cotraveler trying to find his way "back home" just as we are.

One subplot during an early episode of *Star Trek: Voyager* finds Kathryn Janeway expressing to her first officer, Chakotay, the intense burden she carries as the commander of a ship lost in space. In response, Chakotay attempts to put the captain in touch with her animal guide. The mantra he recites expresses hope that "out there" might be "one powerful being" who can give Janeway "the answers she seeks."

Alanis Morissette, Joan Osborne, and Kathryn Janeway express feelings we often sense. When we are honest with ourselves, we admit that our lives just aren't panning out as we hoped they would. Our present reality doesn't quite match the dreams we once had. More significantly, deep inside we feel lost and uncertain about where to turn. We are not even sure what we are lost from or what we are searching for. Although we sense an intense longing within ourselves, when we get right down to it, we can't quite put our finger on what the object of our yearning might in fact be. As a result, we are not at all certain where to look to find the answer to our quest.

As these feelings indicate, we all face the existential question "What am I longing for?" We wonder where we can go to find fulfillment to the yearning desire lodged deep within our being. What response does the Christian faith offer?

The Goal of Our Inner Yearning

In chapter 2 we explored the question, Who am I and why am I here? In that context I spoke about a fundamental human homelessness and how this points to the fact that we are created to be the divine image-bearers. We now return to this basic theme. However, in this chapter we view it from the perspective of the more personal question, What is the fulfillment of the longings I myself feel?

Yet stated in this manner, the question is not formulated quite right. If I were to tell you what I really want, I would quickly discover that my true desires are not exhausted by a list of things I might enumerate. In the end, I find myself admitting that more important than wanting things is my need for relationship. Thus, our existential question shouldn't read, "What am I longing for?" but "Whom am I seeking?"

The Christian answer is, in a word, "God." The fifth-century church theologian Augustine spoke for the entire Christian tradition when he concluded from his own journey, "You have made us for yourself, and our heart is restless until it rests in you."[1]

Douglas Coupland, the best-selling writer who coined the designation "Generation X," confirms Augustine's conclusion.

In his intriguing work *Life after God*, the young author capsulizes the spiritual pilgrimage of the first generation raised "after God"—those who have grown up this side of the demise of the cultural dominance of Christianity and yet who still yearn for the presence of God in their lives.

Coupland's literary odyssey comes to a climax with the author baring his own soul. For one brief moment he has found an openness of heart that he doubts he will ever achieve again. Speaking from the depth of his soul he voices an unexpected confession. "My secret," he writes, "is that I need God—that I am sick and can no longer make it alone."[2]

As Augustine and Coupland suggest, we are on a quest for God. Christians speak of the goal of this journey as "knowing" God. But what does it mean to know God? Is this even possible?

The End of Our Quest

Christians boldly declare that people can indeed know God. As we developed in chapter 5, we believe that Jesus of Nazareth is the revelation of God. Jesus provides the only sure response to Joan Osborne's query "What if God was one of us?" In Jesus we see God, we find God, we come to know God (John 14:7, 9; 17:3).

To many people, however, such talk is sheer nonsense. They are skeptical of any claim to know God, including ours. Such skepticism does harbor a certain truth. It admonishes us to clarify what we mean by our assertion. In saying "we know God" we are not suggesting that we possess complete knowledge about God. We don't know all the ins and outs of God's eternal being. The biblical writers warn against thinking that finite, mortal humans can fully comprehend the infinite, eternal God. For example, the prophet Isaiah says on God's behalf: "As the heavens are higher than the earth, so are my ways higher than your ways and my thoughts than your thoughts" (Isa. 55:9). Rather than professing to know all about God, we are really declaring that we have come to know God.

How so? Is there something we do and thereby know God? No. We don't come to know God through any great discoveries we make ourselves. Instead, in the knowing process God seeks us out. God takes the initiative. God comes to us!

How? By giving us a long list of statements about the divine being and character for us to memorize so that we might prepare to take a destiny-determining exam at the gates of heaven? Hardly! There is a great difference between knowing God and knowing a list of facts about God.

Instead, God initiates the "knowing process" by bringing us into personal relationship. This means that above all, knowing God entails enjoying fellowship with the living God. When we know God in this personal way, we begin to see all the lofty declarations about God for what they really are—verbal vehicles through which we describe the greatness of the one we have come to know.

So knowing God means being brought into fellowship with God. But who is this God? In her poignant song, Joan Osborne raises the crucial question about what God's name would be, if God had a name. We assert that knowing God includes knowing God's name.

Throughout the ages Christians have recited the name of the God we know. The Apostles' Creed summarizes the Christian belief:

> I believe in God the Father . . .
> And in Jesus Christ his only Son, our Lord . . .
> I believe in the Holy Spirit . . .

This ancient confession encapsulates the only ultimate response to the yearnings of "homeless" people. When we come to know God, therefore, we discover that the object of our longings is not a distant Unknown about whom we can only wonder. The great "Whom" in the question "Whom am I longing for?" is the triune God who has become our dear Friend.

The Way to Relationship with God

Viewed from the Christian perspective, the answer to my inner yearnings is the enjoyment of fellowship with the triune

One. Ultimately, therefore, "all I really want" is to know God, but how does this happen? What pathway brings me into this relationship? There is much confusion about this today.

The Erroneous Way of Self-Help. Some of the most confusing voices come from the advertisers of self-help programs. Although these schemes appear to vary, they all tend to be variations on one basic theme. Each claims to offer a means whereby we can discover our own fundamental "godhood."[3]

Why this? The sellers of self-help programs are generally agreed that our root problem is essentially intellectual and not at all moral. What we lack is proper information. We need to open our eyes to see that everything is ultimately good because everything is ultimately God. One self-help seller, Carol Riddell, offered this clarification: "That which is not good, which is evil, is not something different from God—an alternative, inherently evil universal force—but behavior without knowledge of the truth."[4]

These misguided "physicians" of the human soul maintain that we are blind to the truth of our innate divinity and hence of our oneness with God, one another, and the entire cosmos. When we finally accept these truths, the self-help specialists optimistically promise, we will actualize our divine nature, evolve into a higher order of being, and bring salvation to humankind. Again Riddell's voice serves as a blatant example of such erroneous thinking:

> In the search for spirit, the meaning of life is twofold. Firstly, we are trying to discover who we really are—to experience the Divine within. Secondly, we are trying to express what we discover, through our actions in the perceived world. People who are adopting this twofold path as their purpose in life are transcending the stage Homo sapiens, and are the early representatives of a new human development—Homo divinus. The expanded consciousness of Homo divinus will enable us to resolve the problems of our current civilisation.[5]

How can we supposedly accomplish this salvation? The self-help gurus suggest various techniques, but high on everybody's list are meditation and positive thinking. These prac- tices do the trick because they supposedly facilitate an altered state of consciousness in which the participant experiences oneness with ultimate reality.

The Gospel of Divine Grace. In contrast to the message of sal- vation through self-help, Christians proclaim the good news of divine grace extended to us from beyond ourselves. This dis- tinction is crucial.

As we noted in chapter 2, our human problem is not merely ignorance. We are alienated from God, one another, creation, and even ourselves; and this estrangement involves a moral dimension. Left to our own devices we might make some progress, but in the end we are unable to remedy our situation. On our own, we are without hope.

Christians, however, have good news to tell. In the midst of our failure, God extends divine grace—salvation—to us. In chapter 5 we noted that in Jesus, God has overcome our alien- ation. In Christ, God has done what we are incapable of doing. God has acted for us.

How do we come to experience this grace? We must note im- mediately that because it is *God's* grace, we cannot produce it. Because it is God's *grace*—a word that means "unmerited favor"—we cannot earn it or demand it. Salvation, therefore, comes as divine favor extended to us even though we don't de- serve it.

At the same time, divine salvation does not come automa- tically. Automatic grace would only be what the German theologian Dietrich Bonhoeffer called "cheap grace,"[6] grace without cost. Such grace, he added, is worthless, for it fails to see that it cost God his Son. Hence, even though divine grace is God's unmerited favor, we must accept it. We must receive it.

"Wait a minute!" you might be saying at this point. "If Jesus' death fundamentally altered the relationship between God and humankind (as we talked about in chapter 5) and if as a result God graciously extends salvation to us, why must we receive God's salvation? This doesn't sound like grace."

Suppose the President of the United States announces an unconditional amnesty for all incarcerated criminals. Although his declaration inaugurates a new situation, each prison inmate must still accept the President's offer. Each must walk out of the jail!

So too with us. We are at enmity against God. We fear and hate the Creator who loves us. In Jesus, God took the first step to remedy this awful situation. As a result, God is now irrevocably reconciled to us; there is no hostility on God's part. But we still need to be reconciled to God (2 Cor. 5:19–20).

Our Turning to God. Again we ask, however, how does this happen? How do we receive the divine grace? The New Testament writers often use the word *conversion* to refer to our response to God's grace. "Conversion" means literally "turning." Just like the physical act of turning one's face from one direction toward another, this spiritual turning involves both a turning from (repentance) and a turning toward (faith). Like the physical act, it leads to a redirecting (a reorienting) of one's life.

We receive divine grace as we turn from. Specifically, we turn from ourselves—from our old way of thinking, feeling, and living. The turning from self entails a change of mind, an altered opinion of ourselves. We once thought we were basically okay, basically good—not perfect, of course, but decent persons nevertheless. And we saw ourselves as quite self-sufficient: We could handle life on our own.

Turning from self entails having one's complacency shaken. We realize our spiritual poverty. We know that despite our best efforts, we are simply not okay. Similar to the apostle Paul, we even sense deep displeasure, sorrow, perhaps hatred for our failure and for the misguided direction in which our lives were headed (Rom. 7:15). What we sincerely desire is a change, a new beginning (Rom. 7:19; Matt. 5:6).

How can such a new start happen? Not merely through turning from self. We know full well that we cannot make amends for the past. Try as we will, we are incapable of pulling off any truly radical changes. Our yearly ritual of making and quickly breaking New Year's resolutions ought to divest us of any illusions about this.

The "turning" that the biblical writers speak of as conversion, therefore, involves a parallel "turning toward." Above all, we turn toward God. Whereas we had previously set our face away from God, we now turn toward the One who in Christ has loved us and who desires a relationship with us. We entrust ourselves to this God. We redirect or refocus our lives on God. As we do, we find ourselves being reoriented in relationship to the triune God. We commit our lives to Jesus as our Lord, and in so doing, we begin to discover a new desire within us: We now want above all to please God in all we do.

The reorientation involved in turning from self toward God leads also to a turning toward others (Mark 12:28–34; 1 John 4:20). The old self-centered way of living gives way to the desire to follow the example of Jesus, "the man for others." We begin to see people around us as persons whom God loves and for whom Jesus died. As a result, we forsake the old impulse to treat them as means to our goals; instead, we seek to minister to their needs and thereby serve Christ (Matt. 25:40).

This reorientation leads to a turning toward creation as well. Whereas we once saw the world around us as existing primarily for our benefit, we now desire to imitate God by being concerned for all that God has made. We seek to be good stewards (Gen. 2:15) so that God's character might shine through us toward all creation.

Finally, we also experience a new turning toward ourselves, for we come to understand our own true identity as God designed us. We now desire nothing less than to live in accordance with God's goal for human existence. Hence, when we turn away from the old self and toward God, we in fact find our true self. As Jesus said, "Those who want to save their life [self] will lose it, but those who lose their life for my sake will find it" (Matt. 16:25).

The Author of Our Relationship with God

What do I really want? To know—to enjoy fellowship with—God. How can I come to know God? By receiving God's gracious salvation. How do I receive divine grace? By turning—turning from myself and toward God. This is the basic Christian answer to the existential question, What am I longing for, and how do I find it? But there is another detail that needs to be filled in.

Not only is God the one for whom we yearn and the one toward whom we turn, but also the one who empowers the turning itself. This power comes from the third trinitarian Person, the Holy Spirit. In this mysterious process the Spirit moves from being "outside" us to becoming "inside." The Spirit replaces our hostility with peace and authors new, spiritual life in us. Consequently, we enjoy fellowship with God, with one another, and with all creation.

The New Testament writers refer to this process as "regeneration" (Titus 3:5), a metaphorical word that speaks about being "born anew" or "born again" (John 3:1–16). Hence, the Spirit is the agent of a spiritual birth. Just as physical birth endows us with a special relationship to our physical parents, so also our spiritual birth means that we have a special relationship with God. Through the Spirit we become God's spiritual offspring—God's child (John 1:12–13). As a result, we now enjoy the most intimate fellowship possible. The indwelling Spirit brings us to address God with the same name of endearment that Jesus himself spoke—"Abba" (Rom. 8:15; Gal. 4:6)—a word that can't be translated into English but it is somewhat similar to our designation "Dad."

When the Spirit moves into our lives, he begins to transform us. The Spirit's goal is that we come to reflect our true identity as children of our heavenly Father after the pattern of Jesus the Son. To this end, the Spirit provides the ability to choose God's will and thereby to live in accordance with God's purposes in creating us.

The New Testament writers refer to this living according to our design as "freedom" (2 Cor. 3:17). Obviously, such freedom does not mean acting without restraint (Gal. 5:13; James 1:25). Instead, the Spirit liberates us that we might be true disciples of Jesus (John 8:31–32, 36). This includes the freedom to "be for others" (Gal. 5:13) and even to renounce our own prerogatives for the sake of serving others (1 Cor. 9:19; 10:23–24).

The Holy Spirit who engages in this glorious transforming work is not some soupy, sentimental, generic "cosmic love" some people speak about today. The one who brings about such a radical change in us is much more than merely "God's 'eternal communication link with His separated sons,' a bridge back to gentle thoughts, the Great Transformer of Perception from fear to love,"[7] as one writer erroneously suggests.

Instead, the one at work within us is the Spirit of the relationship between the Father and the Son, as we discussed in chapter 4. Consequently, when the Holy Spirit indwells us, the Spirit brings us to participate in the eternal relationship the Son enjoys with the Father, for this relationship is who the Spirit in fact is. For this reason we are the beloved children of our heavenly Father. It is this identity as God's child that ultimately fulfills our deepest longings. No wonder Christians sing, "Amazing grace how sweet the sound."

The Focus of Belonging

One of the most popular TV programs of the 1990s, the sitcom *Friends,* centers on a small group of Gen Xers who share two apartments across the hall from one another. Through thick and thin, good times and bad, these friends laugh with one another, hurt for one another, and support one another. But above everything else the friendship they share gives meaning to each of their lives.

The central message of the series is captured in the program's theme song, "I'll Be There for You." The lyrics express candidly the Gen X experience of life. The verse relates how reality is so often a far cry from what we were led to anticipate. The chorus, however, expresses the group members' promise always to be "there" for one another. Why? Because, to cite the last line of the song, "you're there for me too."

The popularity of *Friends* reminds us that we are social creatures. In our quest to discover what we really want, it doesn't take long before we turn away from things to people. Ultimately, we hope to find what can satisfy the deep yearning within us in relationships with others. Why? Because our deepest desire isn't to possess things but to belong. This leads us to seek out friendships that (we hope) can provide us with the sense of "belonging" we crave.

This "turn to relationships" is not misguided. The yearning we sense—the emptiness or homelessness we feel inside us—simply can't be filled by the abundance of our possessions. Where we go astray, however, is in the poor relationship choices we make. We often look for belonging in the wrong places. Think of how many people (of all ages) have messed up their lives by getting hooked up with the "wrong crowd." Although these relationships promised to provide a sense of belonging, in the end they only deepened the feeling of isolation.

As we have seen, the ultimate place where we can find genuine belonging is in relationship to God. The One for whom we are yearning is the triune God. Nevertheless, there is more to the story. Although we know God and are known by God personally, we do not receive the divine grace that brings us into relationship with God solely as individuals. Rather, knowing God is closely linked to participation in a particular group. According to the New Testament, the most important group is the community of Christ's disciples—the church.

"The church?" you might reiterate in disbelief. Perhaps you are one of the many people who have never really thought of the church as providing answers to life's questions. You may sense that a great gulf separates you from the church, or at least the church as you surmise it must be.

The distance from the church many people feel was vividly portrayed in a series of installments of the comic strip "Betty." Out of curiosity, the couple's teenage son had begun to read the old, never opened, family Bible. As a result, he told his parents that he wanted to be baptized. Having no religious background whatever, the parents arbitrarily chose a church from the Yellow Pages. In the prebaptism interview, the pastor informed them that for the sake of this event they should choose a godparent for their son. Faced with this daunting task, Betty realized that no one they knew was at all religious. In fact, she could think of only one of their acquaintances who even wore a cross—her husband's freewheeling brother.

The situation of Betty and her family is all too typical today. But why is it so? This widespread sense of disconnectedness is in part the result of mistaken ideas about the church. One prevalent misconception is closely tied to the individualistic character of our society. Many people mistake the church for an organization—similar to a country club or a civic group (like Kiwanis)—that a person can join at will. Sometimes churches even contribute to this misconception by the cavalier manner in which they solicit members and donations.

But the church is not merely an organization. It is not a conglomerate of individuals who have simply chosen to associate with one another. Consequently, the role of the church in our quest for belonging is actually quite different from what many people at first surmise. It begins already at the process of turning from self toward God we talked about earlier.

Belonging to a New Community

We spoke already of the receiving of divine grace as a turning from self toward God. We indicated that this involves the Holy Spirit who transforms our lives, but the process includes another dimension as well. The church is intimately involved in this act of turning.

What may come immediately to mind is the role of the church in proclaiming the Christian message to those who have not heard it before. Of course, this is an important aspect of the church's mission, but the role I have in mind lies much deeper than this. In the transformation the biblical writers call "conversion," we come to see ourselves from a new vantage point— from the vista of a new community, the church. In this manner, the church functions as our new "community of reference." Let me explain this somewhat "heady" yet very practical concept.

Each of us views ourselves, others, and the world from a specific perspective. At the heart of this perspective is a set of basic categories, beliefs, or fundamental ways of speaking, which together comprise what we may call our "interpretive framework." Each of us brings this interpretive framework to our lives. Through it we experience, make sense of, and speak about ourselves and the world we inhabit.

This interpretive framework is especially crucial to our sense of who we are (our "personal identity"). As we noted in chapter 2, we all must answer the question, Who am I? But in what manner do we articulate our answer? Most of us tend to say who we are by "telling our story."

The story we tell, however, isn't simply a chronicle of every minute incident that has happened since we were born. (Who would have the time to listen to the entire narrative?) Instead, we organize the diverse aspects of our lives into what we see as a meaningful whole. We bring the isolated events of our lives together through a plot line, but we don't make up this plot ourselves. Instead, we use borrowed categories to create the plot that gives us our sense of self. These categories come from the social groups (or communities) in which we participate.

In short, my sense of who I am is determined to a great extent by the group of which I am a member. This, in fact, is one of the central themes of the sitcom *Friends*. Now let's see how this insight helps us understand the role of the church in conversion.

Turning from self and toward God entails a reinterpretation of who we are. It involves the introduction of a new plot line into our personal story. We "borrow" the categories for this plot from the biblical story of God's saving action toward humankind as told by the church.

Like other Christians, we begin to speak the biblical language of the "old life" and "the new" in keeping with Paul's statement "Therefore, if anyone is in Christ, there is a new creation: the old has gone, the new has come!" (2 Cor. 5:17). We testify to the same experience as the hymn writer John Newton, who in turn drew his lyrics from images found in the New Testament:

> I once was lost but now am found,
> Was blind but now I see.

Although the details vary from Christian to Christian, the basic plot is the same. It speaks about the errors and failure of the past that have been overcome through an encounter with Jesus Christ.

Just as we reinterpret our lives through the lenses of the biblical story, so also we view others and the world differently from before. We now look at every aspect of life through "Christian" eyes.

But note what this means. By reinterpreting our story in this manner we are accepting the story of the Christian community as our own. Hence, we have become part of a new people, the Christian community. And in providing us with this new set of categories, the church has provided the sense of belonging we really want.

The church functions in several other dimensions of our "turning" as well. In addition to giving us a new framework for viewing ourselves and the world, the Christian message embodies a new set of values. In turning toward God we come to accept these values, especially the values Jesus exemplified, as our own. We desire to live out these values—peace, justice, patience, but above all love—in our attitudes and actions. This not only marks each of us individually as a disciple of Jesus, it unites us with the community of disciples who share the same values and the same desire to live according to them.

Turning from self toward God also marks a change of loyalty: from self to God in Christ. Loyalties, however, are never purely personal; an allegiance always links us with those who share it. So also the change in loyalty involved in our turning toward God brings us together with others. By renouncing our fundamental allegiance to self and pledging our fidelity to Jesus, we become part of a new community, the fellowship of all who declare "Jesus is Lord." This new community, in turn, becomes the people to whom we belong, and together with them we belong to God.

Belonging to a People in Relationship

This observation leads us quite directly to another aspect of the church and its role in our finding true "belonging." We noted that turning toward God involves a new loyalty.

Although this new allegiance is "vertical"—it binds us to God—it also inaugurates a "horizontal" bond. Allegiance to Christ unites all those who share the same fundamental loyalty. But this bond is more than merely the sense of oneness that arises when we realize that each of us in our own little way "loves Jesus." Rather, our common allegiance to God and our shared love for Jesus forge in us a deep commitment to one another as well. I pledge that I will indeed be there for you, and I know that you are there for me too.

How does this happen? How do we come to be committed to one another? How do we become a people in relationship? The answer is: through the Holy Spirit. We may view this from a couple of angles.

One perspective builds from the idea of family we noted earlier. When we turn from self toward God, the Spirit brings us into relationship with God as our heavenly Father. But this is not ours as isolated persons. Instead, because each of us is a child of God, we are related to one another. We are sisters and brothers—a family. The Spirit births us into a new family. As a family, we are a people in relationship and a people who are committed to one another.

The same conclusion arises from another slant as well. In turning us away from self and toward God, the Spirit draws us out of our alienation into a reconciled relationship with God. However, the biblical writers clearly teach that our estrangement from God taints all our relationships. Because we have made ourselves God's enemies, we experience isolation—we are closed in on ourselves—as well as alienation from one another, from creation around us, and even from our own true being. The Father sent the Son and gave us the Holy Spirit not only so that we might enjoy reconciliation with God but also so that all our relationships might be healed. In turning us toward God, therefore, the Spirit also draws us out of our isolation into wholesome relationships with one another. In so doing, he transforms us from a collection of individuals into a people. We become "one body," to use Paul's preferred designation.

As the company of those who have received the divine

grace, therefore, the church is far more than a collection of "saved" individuals. We are a people committed both to God and to one another. We are a community, a people among whom we find true belonging.

But we have not yet mentioned the most foundational dimension of the church as a people whom the Spirit draws together into a community of "belonging." In chapter 4 we indicated that because God is the triune One—Father, Son, and Holy Spirit—God is love. In our answer to the question "Who am I?" in chapter 2, we declared that God's goal for us is that we be the image of God, that is, that we reflect the divine nature (love). Now we must add: According to the New Testament, God wills that the church be a people who show what God is like. God desires that by being a loving community who reflect God's character we shine as God's image-bearers.

How? Again, the answer is "Through the Holy Spirit." We have noted repeatedly that through our turning to God the Spirit makes us God's children. But this is exactly the relationship Jesus the Son enjoys with the one he called "Father." By causing us to become the brothers and sisters of Christ, the Spirit brings us to share in the love the Son enjoys with the Father. In this manner, we participate in the love that lies at the very heart of the triune God!

Participation in God's eternal love, however, is not ours as individuals in isolation. It is a privilege we share. The Spirit's goal, in fact, is to bring us together into one people who participate together in the love of God and who by their loving relationships show God's great love to all.

Consequently, unlike what TV sitcoms propagate, the church is not merely a group of friends who happen to share common experiences or even who happen to speak a common language. The church is a community of believers who because they participate together in the Holy Spirit share together in the eternal communion between the Father and the Son. Ultimately this is why God calls us to be a people committed to one another. We are to be a community of divine love, a people bound together by the love present among us through God's Spirit. As a result, we find here true belonging.

Although the words may be a bit archaic, Christians nevertheless still find great meaning in John Fawcett's old hymn:

> Blest be the tie that binds
> Our hearts in Christian love;
> The fellowship of kindred minds
> Is like to that above.
>
> When we asunder part,
> It gives us inward pain;
> But we shall still be joined in heart,
> And hope to meet again.[8]

Affirming Our Belonging

One of my fond childhood memories is of the grand Fourth of July celebrations I experienced on the prairies. I recall how in early evening we would pack into the grandstand at the fairgrounds. We would listen to the community band play John Phillip Sousa marches—"Stars and Stripes Forever" was my favorite—while we eagerly anticipated dusk. When it finally grew dark enough, the show would begin. Fireworks! First overhead. Then in the grassy baseball playing field. Then once again in the sky above us. Adults would "oo" and "ah." Babies would cry. But I would watch without uttering a sound, mesmerized by the display. The evening always came to a climax with a seemingly endless shower of aerial bursts. And then, when the noise subsided, the most glorious sight of all: deep in center field the fiery representation of the American flag. How could we not join the band in a heartfelt rendition of "The Star Spangled Banner"?

What was going on at these events that made them so memorable? We were celebrating the fact that we were a community. By being there together, we were reaffirming that we belonged.

So also in the church. Our sense that "we belong" is strengthened by certain symbolic acts that vividly portray our belonging to God and God's family. Although we do this in many ways, two acts stand out: baptism and the Lord's Supper.

The Acts of Belonging. Many Christians refer to baptism and the Lord's Supper as "sacraments." In the ancient world this word referred to the oath (*sacramentum*) of fidelity and obedience to the commanding officer a Roman soldier would swear upon enlisting in the army. Other Christians prefer to designate these acts "ordinances" (from the verb *to ordain*), in keeping with the belief that Jesus himself commanded his faithful disciples to practice them. Taken together the two terms remind us that Christ has given baptism and the Lord's Supper to us as symbols of our relationship to God and one another. Hence, we might simply call them "acts of belonging."

Baptism and the Lord's Supper contribute to our "belonging" in two related ways. They testify to God's grace and to our reception of that grace. The acts of belonging do this because of their link to the biblical story, the drama of salvation as it focuses on Jesus. They are symbolic reminders of the past events through which God extended divine grace toward us. Specifically, they declare that Jesus died to reconcile us to God and that he rose from the dead to give us new life. These acts speak about the future as well, reminding us that Jesus will return one day.

The acts of belonging don't merely remind us of this great biblical drama, however. Through them we symbolically participate in God's saving acts. In a sense, baptism and the Lord's Supper transport us into the past. Through them, we declare that Jesus died and rose again for us, and as we do so, we place ourselves into Jesus' story. At the same time, we reenact our turning from self toward God. Through this reenactment the Holy Spirit confirms our new identity as God's children.

These acts transport us into the future as well. Through baptism and the Lord's Supper we celebrate that great day when Jesus will return in glory and we will be transformed into his likeness. As we anticipate that day in this symbolic manner, the Holy Spirit etches this vision on our hearts and strengthens us to live out the vision in the here and now.

Both acts vividly portray our belonging. Yet because they are distinctive they do so in different ways.

Declaring That We Belong. Simply stated, baptism involves a representative of the church applying water to someone in the name of the triune God. Yet this seemingly mundane act carries great meaning. It symbolizes the gaining of a new identity through our turning from self toward God. For this reason, baptism is a type of initiation into our new life as a child of God and a participant in Christ's church. This act declares that we belong to God and to a new community—God's family.

Baptism symbolizes our belonging, for through it we give symbolic expression to the new plot line of our "story." The act declares that through our connection with Jesus' death and resurrection for us, we have died to our old self and our old way of living so that we might now live "in newness of life" (Rom. 6:3–8). In so doing, baptism also declares that we belong to Christ's people, for as Paul declared, we are baptized "into Christ's body," the church (1 Cor. 12:13). Hence, we share the same story as all others who have been baptized. We have become part of the community that is defined by the story of Jesus' life, death, and resurrection.

In addition, baptism symbolizes our belonging by declaring symbolically that we have changed our allegiance. In baptism, we announce for all to hear that we have turned from self and the devil in order to pledge ourselves to God (1 Peter 3:21). In so doing, baptism declares that we are now part of the community in which Jesus reigns as Lord.

Baptism likewise declares "we belong" because it is God's promise of our glorious future. Jesus' story (which we commemorate in baptism) did not end with his death and resurrection. Instead, he ascended to "the right hand of the Father" (Rom. 8:34; Eph. 1:20; Heb. 1:3) and will one day return in glory. So also through baptism we anticipate joining Christ in his resurrection (Rom. 8:11; 1 Cor. 15:51–57). To this end, baptism symbolizes the coming of the Spirit, whose presence in our lives is God's pledge of our future resurrection (Rom. 8:11; 2

Cor. 1:22; 5:5; Eph. 1:13, 14) and of our complete transformation after the pattern of Christ (2 Cor. 1:22; 5:5; Eph. 1:14).

As a declaration that "we belong," baptism ought to be a day to remember. Memories of our baptism should continually remind us how one day "long ago" the Holy Spirit brought us into relationship with God and God's people. Every baptism we witness ought to remind us of our corporate responsibility to nurture all who belong to God's family, as well as of the challenge we share to proclaim the good news to the many in the world who have not yet come to belong to the new community.

Reaffirming Our Belonging. One ongoing way we remember our baptism is through participation in the other act of belonging, the Lord's Supper. This act repeatedly reaffirms that we belong to God and God's family.

Like baptism, the Lord's Supper speaks about our belonging through its connection with the biblical story of Jesus. In keeping with our Lord's command, "Do this in remembrance of me," we commemorate not only Jesus' last meal with his disciples but also his sacrificial death for us to which that meal pointed. Thus, the bread speaks of the giving of his body, and the wine represents the shedding of his blood. As we eat and drink these elements, we portray as well the great mystery of belonging to Christ: Just as ingesting food sustains physical life, so also our connection with Christ through his death and resurrection is the source of spiritual vitality. By eating and drinking, therefore, we publicly reaffirm our spiritual act of turning to God.

We noted earlier that the biblical drama stretches from the past into the future. When he ordained the memorial meal, our Lord spoke a promise about that future: "I tell you, I will never again drink of this fruit of the vine until that day when I drink it new with you in my Father's kingdom" (Matt. 26:29). As a result, the Lord's Supper is a reminder that there is more to come. Through our participation in this act, we claim his promise and anticipate the day when we will enjoy the fullness of belonging to Christ and one another in God's eternal community.

Through the Lord's Supper we also reaffirm the pledge made at baptism. Just as in baptism we publicly announce our change of allegiance, presence at the Lord's Supper symbolizes that we do indeed belong to God through Jesus our Lord (1 Cor. 10:21). By eating and drinking together, we reaffirm that as Christ's disciples we belong to one another. Our fundamental unity finds symbolic expression in the one loaf of bread we share (1 Cor. 10:17).

The Task We Share

Baptism and the Lord's Supper vividly portray our belonging to God and one another. Through our participation in these acts of belonging we celebrate—and reaffirm—our belonging to Christ's community. But there is one additional dimension to all this. God has brought us together for a purpose. We have something to do. And as we engage in our shared task, we discover that our sense of belonging is deepened.

This task has three foundational dimensions.

Being a Worshiping Community. Humans seem to be natural-born worshipers. Yet not everything that goes by the name can in fact be called true worship. In his theological discussion with a Samaritan woman over a cup of water, Jesus declared that the day would come when "the true worshipers will worship the Father in spirit and truth" (John 4:23). That day is now. Our task is to be a community of true worshipers (1 Cor. 14:26; Heb. 10:25). But what is true worship?

The word itself means attributing worth to the one who is worthy.[9] This suggests that for worship to be true it must be correctly focused, that is, directed toward the only true God.

Who is this God? The true God is the Holy One (Ps. 29:2; 96:8; 1 Chron. 16:29) to whom the angels continually direct their praise as they sing, "Holy, holy, holy, the Lord God Almighty, who was and is and is to come" (Rev. 4:6–8; Isa. 6:3). The God who is worthy of praise is also the Creator. Hence, the twenty-four elders of the book of Revelation declare, "You are worthy, our Lord and God, to receive glory and honor and power, for you created all things, and by your will they existed and were created" (Rev. 4:11). But above all, the true God is the One who has acted for our salvation and extended grace toward us.

We engage in our task to be a worshiping community, therefore, as we offer our praise to the only true God, the triune One. Fundamentally, we direct our worship to the Father, but we praise the Son as well, for he is "worthy . . . to receive . . . honor and glory and praise!" (Rev. 5:12, NIV). We also honor the Holy Spirit who brings us into relationship with the Father through the Son.

In addition, true worship is worship that is truly offered to God. We bring our praise to God in many ways. For example, we can verbalize it (Heb. 13:15). We can declare God's greatness and goodness (1 Chron. 16:9, 23; Ps. 95:1; 96:2–3; 1 Peter 2:9).

Similarly, we can praise God through music. Because music captures feelings, emotion, and mood, through music we can offer God these dimensions of our response to divine grace, such as the joy we share as reconciled people (Ps. 95:1; 92:1, 4).

We can also praise God through prayer. In prayer we honor and extol God (adoration). We acknowledge our failure and voice our agreement that it is displeasing in God's sight (confession). We express our gratitude for all that God has done and is doing (thanksgiving). We bring our concerns and needs to God, asking for divine provision to meet these needs (supplication).

By focusing our attention on the majestic God, true worship lifts our sights about the mundane aspects of life that so noisily clamor for our attention. For this reason, our corporate worship ought to be an exhilarating experience. An avid skier was right in comparing "church"—that is, the gathering of the worshiping community—with his experience of being in the Vallée Blanche in the Chamonix area of France:

> The valley is a huge, vaulted space, the floor of God's winter palace, a dwarfing place, a place so unrelentingly breathtaking that you have to find a bar or cafe at the bottom in order to sit down, gather your thoughts and reassess your importance in the universe. It's what going to church is supposed to be like.[10]

Being a Nurturing Community. The evening before he died, Jesus engaged in what people of his day considered the most menial task imaginable: He washed the feet of the twelve disciples (John 13:1–11). Then he commanded them to follow his example (John 13:12–17). In this manner, our Lord indicated that we are to be a nurturing community.

Not only are we to be there for one another but, even more importantly, we are to engage actively in one another's lives in such a manner that we build one another up, so that each of us might become spiritually mature (Eph. 4:11–13). Thus, we seek to minister to those who are plagued with material or spiritual needs. We share the burdens of those who are facing difficulties (Gal. 6:1–2). We encourage and admonish those who are stumbling (Heb. 10:24–25). We nurture those who are "weak" in the faith (Rom. 14:1, 19).

In addition, we sense an accountability to one another. We take seriously the simple truth that we are interdependent. We know that what each of us does affects the others. Because we realize that every member of the community can be an instrument of the Spirit's work in fostering maturity in us, we are open to being instructed, admonished, and encouraged by one another.

Being an Outward-Directed Community. A sense of true belonging simply can't be kept to oneself. Consequently, Christians long to see the whole human family reconciled to God, one another, and creation. Our concern for others quite naturally moves beyond the boundaries of our own community. For this reason, we direct our energies toward bringing others to enjoy the belonging we have found.

One focus of our efforts is what many Christians call "evangelism." Our first inclination when we hear this word may be to think of that young person with a gospel tract we once encountered on a beach in California. Of course, evangelism does involve the various ways in which Christians proclaim the good news of God's grace (Matt. 24:14; Mark 1:15; Rom. 10:14). Why do we do this? Simply because we long to have others hear the message so that they might turn from self toward God and experience with us the joy of belonging to God and God's family. For this reason, we untiringly tell and retell "the old, old story of Jesus and his love."

But there is another dimension to evangelism as well. Our life together is in a certain sense itself a "proclamation" of the good news. For example, as we gather to offer our praises, we are implicitly admonishing others to turn away from the worship of false gods of all types and to join us in the worship of the true God that one day will reverberate throughout the universe. Further, as we seek to be there for one another and to nurture one another in the faith, we are unconsciously inviting others to forsake relationships that we know will ultimately prove unsatisfying so that they might find the true sense of belonging available in relationship with God and God's family.

While evangelism is a crucial aspect of our outward-oriented task, our mission in the world is not limited to the expansion of the church's boundaries. It also includes service to the world.

In serving others, we take our cue from Jesus himself, who felt compassion for the hungry, the sick, the outcasts, and the demon-possessed. As Christ's body—that is, his presence in the world—we follow our Lord's example. We desire to display the compassion and love that characterized our Lord. This desire leads us quite naturally to bind the wounds of the injured and outcast of the world, after the pattern of the Good Samaritan (Luke 10:25–37).

Because we know that reconciliation with God must be embodied in all our relationships, we seek to be instruments of the Holy Spirit in bringing reconciliation to our world. This leads us to seek to change social structures that wound people. We desire that all such vehicles of human interaction reflect to an increasing extent the principles of justice and righteousness taught in the Bible.

What am I searching for? I am yearning to know God, that is, to belong to God and to God's family. Where do I look for the end of my longings? Not in relationships and friendships that can't bring ultimate satisfaction or an ultimate sense of belonging. Instead I can find the goal of my quest only by turning from self toward the triune God as I leave behind my old identity and discover who I am created to be within the fellowship of the community of Christ. As I do so, I will find that this is indeed all I really want.

NOTES

1. Augustine, *Confessions* 1.1, trans. John K. Ryan (New York: Doubleday Image Books, 1960), 43.
2. Douglas Coupland, *Life after God* (New York: Pocket Books, 1994), 359.
3. See, for example, Rodney R. Romney, *Journey to Inner Space: Finding God-in-Us* (Nashville: Abingdon, 1980), 26.
4. Carol Riddell, *The Findhorn Community* (Findhorn, Scotland: Findhorn Press, 1990), 30–31.
5. Riddell, *Findhorn Community,* 25.
6. Dietrich Bonhoeffer, *The Cost of Discipleship,* trans. R. H. Fuller and Irmgard Booth, revised edition (New York: Macmillan, 1963), 45–48.
7. Marianne Williamson, *A Return to Love* (New York: HarperCollins, 1992), 34.
8. John Fawcett, "Blest Be the Tie That Binds."
9. *Worship* may be defined as: "To pay divine honors to; to reverence with supreme respect and veneration; to perform religious service to; to adore; to idolize." *New Webster's Dictionary of the English Language* (Delair, 1971), 1148.
10. Neil Stibbins, "The World on High," *Ski* (January 1995): 120.

Chapter 7

Is the World—
Am I—Going Anywhere?

*I*n March 1997 thirty-nine members of a group known as the Heaven's Gate staged a bizarre mass suicide in an affluent community near San Diego, California. The cult members apparently believed that by taking their lives they would rendezvous with a spaceship hiding in the tail of comet Hale-Bopp, which was passing by Earth. The spaceship would then transport the faithful cult members to heaven.[1]

Meanwhile a published poll revealed that Canadians, who according to the United Nations Human Development Index live in what the rest of the world finds to be the most desirable place on earth, are in fact "in the grip of unprecedented national despair." The poll respondents indicated that the citizens of this singular blessed land "foresee a grim future" and that they have given up on traditional institutions, such as government.[2]

In differing ways these news stories bring to the surface a single reality, the uncertainty that has increasingly come to characterize our society. People today are simply not convinced that life—whether their personal lives or life on this planet—goes anywhere.

Even Charlie Brown has been infected with the virus of gloom. A November 1995 installment of the popular comic strip "Peanuts" finds the melancholy lad lying in his bed with his faithful dog Snoopy on his lap. Charlie Brown reports to the snoozing puppy that he sometimes lies awake asking whether his generation can look to the future with hope. Gripped with despondency, the boy then relates how a voice comes to him out of the dark that at first responds confidently but soon changes its tune to a hesitant it-sort-of-depends.

Two hundred years ago the German philosopher Immanuel Kant noted that humans must come to grips with three central questions: What can I know? What should I do? And what can I hope for?[3] Kant's third query has emerged as *the* crucial question of our day. What does the Christian gospel have to say to this situation? Do Christians offer a relevant response to Kant's third question? In short, is the world—and am I—going anywhere?

Beyond Death's Door:
I Know Where I'm Going

Kant's question "What can I hope for?" is especially relevant for us as individuals. "What can I hope for, for my own life?" Most of us face this question in earnest when we are confronted with our own death, when we come to realize that we too will one day die. "Can I hope for anything beyond death?" we ask.

The answers we hear today are often negative. For example, in his novel *Herzog,* Saul Bellow probed one typical response to the question: "This generation thinks—and this is its thought of thoughts—that nothing faithful, vulnerable, fragile can be durable or have any true power. Death waits for these things as a cement floor waits for a dropping light bulb."[4]

Although written in the early 1960s, Bellow's appraisal expresses the feelings of many people today as well. Death—the certainty that I will die—casts a gloomy shadow over life. People wonder if a life that will end in certain death is worth living. For them, the reality of death produces a menacing, existential angst.

For others, however, death looms as an attractive alternative to life and life's uncertainties. Members of apocalyptic cults like Heaven's Gate strongly feel the pull of death. The courting of death is especially evident among young people. A 1995 survey of preteens in the USA suggests that the era of carefree childhood is quickly coming to an end. The poll portrays children as harboring a host of what previous generations would have viewed as quite "grown-up" anxieties. Kids today fear not only doing poorly in school but also being victimized by AIDS, poverty, death, kidnapping, and physical or sexual abuse.[5] As these children enter their teenage years, additional fears surface, ranging from the fear of becoming the targets of teen-on-teen violence to anxiety in the face of economic insecurity in a world of bleak economic prospects.

As a result, an increasing number of youth are turning to the ultimate "way out": suicide—which having tripled in the three decades between 1962 and 1992[6] has risen to be the leading cause of death among North American teens. On October 7, 1994, three eighteen-year-old young men drove a 1987 Plymouth across Canada. Their journey ended inside a locker at the Mini Storage near Vancouver, B.C. With the locker door tightly closed and the car engine running, it didn't take long for the trio to succumb to carbon monoxide poisoning. They died with the music of Kurt Cobain's band Nirvana wailing from the car's cassette player. Left behind was a sixty-page suicide journal. Bearing the ominous title "The Last Trip," the script ended with the telling words, "We have lived our lives and this life is not for us—goodbye."[7]

So widespread is public awareness of suicide's lure that fans of pop singer Jann Arden interpreted her haunting song about heartbreak "Will You Remember Me" (1993) as an ode to suicide. The singer reported even receiving a letter from a suicidal girl who bought the recording to leave to her parents, "because she just didn't see any point in living."[8]

So what is the answer to our culture's ambiguous fixation with death? Is death the angst-producing darkness that casts its chilling shadow over life? Does it instead fulfill its promise to provide a nihilistic escape from a world spinning out of control or from a treadmill life weighted down with meaningless tasks and unsatisfying relationships? And what—if anything—

awaits us beyond death's door? What hope is there in the face of death?

Life beyond Death?

Death, as we all know, is universal. All people eventually die. As the Hebrew sage who wrote the book of Ecclesiastes concluded centuries before the birth of Jesus: "The same fate comes to all, to the righteous and the wicked, to the good and the evil, to the clean and the unclean, to those who offer sacrifices and those who do not." They all "go to the dead" (Eccl. 9:2–3).

What is this death that eventually overcomes each of us? We might, of course, limit our answer to the obvious. It entails the cessation of biological functioning. But when we probe deeper into our psyche, we sense that it is much more. Death, we realize, seems to mark the end of personal life. Or to state the matter more sharply, I will die, and my death threatens to spell the end of *my* existence.

Viewed in this sense, death looms mysterious. It is perhaps the greatest mystery of human existence. As a result, it strikes us as gravely ominous. Death marks a fall into isolation, a loss of identity, and as such a breach of community.

This uneasy attitude toward death is not unique to our time. It has plagued nearly every people and every civilization. The ancient Hebrews, for example, felt a similar ambiguity. On the one hand, they saw death in part as the inevitable result of the aging process (1 Sam. 3:6). Thus, they believed that to die "old and full of years" is one of the highest blessings God could bestow. And death meant simply to be "gathered" to one's "people" (Gen. 49:33).

On the other hand, the Hebrews also sensed that death stands in sharp contrast to life. Whereas life is connected with God (1 Sam. 2:6; Job 1:21), death is an evil, alien power over which humans have no control (2 Sam. 22:6; Ps. 89:48). To die, therefore, is to descend into a shadowy, silent realm called Sheol (Job 21:13; Ps. 55:15; 115:17; Prov. 15:24; Ezek. 31:15–17)[9] where no one can praise or see God (Ps. 6:5; Isa. 38:10–11). In the face of death understood in this manner, the Hebrews could find only a glimmer of hope (Job 14:14).

Existence—But in What Form?

In the materialistic modern era, some people concluded confidently that nothing lies beyond death's door. When you die, you die. Death simply ends it all. Most people today, however, find this viewpoint increasingly unsatisfying. They cling to the possibility that something lies beyond death. They want to believe that somehow we survive death; somehow we pass through death into a realm on the other side.

What lies beyond death's door? What is this great "beyond" like? Here opinions vary.

Monism. Suppose the experience of individual existence that characterizes our life on earth is—contrary to empirical evidence—in fact unreal. Suppose further that at death our eyes are opened to see this mirage. Suppose that through death we lose our personal identity—our sense of individualization, our very self—as we mesh into the all-encompassing Unity.

If these suppositions are correct, then death leads to the dissolution of human personal distinctions as well as the loss of all distinction between God and creatures. Just as a drop of water disappears into the vast ocean, so also we mesh into the great All. This view is often called "monism."

Although typical of Eastern religions such as Hinduism, monism has become increasingly popular in the West as well. For example, James Redfield's runaway best-selling "novel" *The Celestine Prophecy* advocates a type of monism. Near the end of the book, one of the characters, who had developed a keen understanding of the truths recorded in the secret book of wisdom referred to as "the Manuscript," dies. Actually, what the book's heroes who watch the event actually see is his image becoming hazy until he finally disappears.

Through the leading female character, Julia, Redfield then offers his own vision of the life beyond. We are headed to a world of incredible beauty and energy. In this realm we experience increased connection with the world itself and with its beauty. This "Heaven," Julia (and hence Redfield) adds, "is already before us. We just can't see it yet." Nevertheless, it remains the goal toward which we are even now evolving.[10]

Not only has the monist vision struck a chord among "pop" writers like Redfield, it also has colored the thinking of some Christians. In what is perhaps her most influential book, *Sexism and God-Talk,* Rosemary Radford Ruether spoke of God as the "great collective personhood . . . in which our achievements and failures are gathered up, assimilated into the fabric of being, and carried forward into new possibilities." Death, in turn, is "the final relinquishment of individuated ego into the great matrix of being."[11]

Despite monism's great attraction, it hides a fatal flaw. The monist vision looks to a realm beyond death in which all personal distinctions—all differentiations between individual humans as well as the distinction between humans and God—evaporate. By declaring that individual existence is ultimately illusionary, monism devalues the personal nature of human life. And it denies the personal character of God as well.

Ironically monism also destroys the foundation for fellowship among humans. According to this erroneous view, true fellowship can only be achieved through the loss of personhood. Christians, in contrast, find the transcendent foundation for the human experience of community in the fellowship of the trinitarian Persons that characterizes the divine life, as we noted in chapter 4. For this reason, we understand true community as the fellowship of persons who bring their distinctiveness, uniqueness, and individuality to the whole. By denying ultimacy to personal life—and hence to personhood—monism undercuts any such vision of community as the fellowship of persons.

Reincarnation. Suppose instead that at death we do not immediately blend into the all-encompassing Unity, the one enveloping Consciousness. Suppose we reemerge in a new earthly form, thereby taking the next step in an indefinitely continuing chain of rebirths designed to foster spiritual growth and progress eventually leading to perfection.

If we opt for this understanding, we have embraced an idea known as "reincarnation."

Although reincarnation was once thought to be the exclusive domain of Eastern religions such as Hinduism, today an increasing number of people—whose ranks include celebrities such as Shirley MacClaine—hold to this teaching. Many even testify that they retain a knowledge of their former personae. To cite one example: Laurel Phelan, who lives in the West Coast city of Vancouver, B.C., claims that her fifty plus past lives, which stretch back to the time of the cavemen, include being the Guinevere of the Camelot legend. Through "past-life regression therapy" Phelan believes she can even experience Guinevere's emotional highs and lows.[12]

Despite its newfound popularity, reincarnation is not a new idea. Rather, the concept dates at least to ancient Greece. In the fourth century before Christ, the philosopher Plato developed an elaborate intellectual defense of the theory that the soul migrates through a series of embodied states on its journey to eternal bliss. Plato also believed that in the present life we can uncover at least some of the knowledge we acquired during our former earthly lives.[13]

Strictly speaking, reincarnation is not a comprehensive theory of life after death. Taken by itself, it does not say how and where—or even if—the journey of successive embodiments ends. The series of rebirths might just as easily go on indefinitely in a never-ending cycle of rebirth—death—rebirth. If we are in this manner trapped on an eternal roller-coaster, which we can never get off, if we are condemned to relive in perpetuity our personal *Groundhog Day*, to cite the popular movie of the early 1990s, with no hope of a way out, then life truly is meaningless.

Most proponents of reincarnation do believe that the process eventually leads somewhere. Many understand its goal in purely monist terms. According to their understanding, the intent of our successive lives is to gain knowledge and attain inner peace. When this happens, we shed our personal identity and are enveloped in the great Unity. Seen in this context, reincarnation is merely the means to the attainment of the final purpose of oneness with the "Great Consciousness." Obviously, it is simply monism in another guise and therefore burdened with the liabilities that haunt monism.

The theory of reincarnation comes up short in other ways as well. It fails to give sufficient seriousness to earthly, bodily existence. Lying behind reincarnation is the assumption that the real person is not the flesh-and-blood, embodied human but the nonphysical soul that migrates from body to body. Hence, rather than seeing the body as an integral part of our essential humanness, this theory reduces each embodied existence to being the vehicle through which the eternal soul functions during the present phase of its journey. This readily risks deprecating the body and physical existence.

Further, by teaching that any specific embodied existence is but a stage in the development of the soul that transcends it, reincarnation fails to give eternal significance to the individual human person. Rather than each human life being important, the theory of reincarnation places the focus on the migrating soul. In its quest for spiritual growth, this soul passes through several such embodied lives, shedding each in turn as a snake sheds successive skins as it grows.

The Bliss of the Immortal Soul. The desire to give individual human existence its due leads many people to a third attractive theory about what happens at death. According to this view, at death the soul discards the body that housed it. Freed from the body, the soul is finally able to attain eternal blessedness. This view presupposes an idea we might call "the immortality of the soul."

Several of the ancient Greek philosophers taught a similar view. In fact, the classic statement depicting death as the doorway to the immortal soul's enjoyment of eternal bliss came in Plato's description of Socrates' death in his dialogue *Phaedo*. Through the mouth of his illustrious student, Socrates explained to his companions that death merely completes the process of liberation begun through philosophical reflection. Death frees the soul from the contaminating influences of the body so that it might attain to the higher realm and apprehend eternal truth.[14]

This Platonic idea has gained a new lease on life through contemporary accounts of "near death experiences."[15] Persons declared clinically dead but who then are revived often report how they had been lifted above their body and ushered into a realm beyond earthly existence.

Consider Chris Lovelidge's testimony: Suffering the excruciating pain of food poisoning contracted through eating contaminated shrimp, he suddenly found himself in another place. "It was just as real as the one I had left," he later reported, "except that it was in a very brightly lit open space near the top of a hill looking down into a valley with beautiful green grass and green trees with a fence running down the centre of this valley." The valley was occupied by shrouded "beings of light." Lovelidge claims he was aware of an overwhelming sense of love and of somehow communicating with the beings. But his experience did not last an eternity. Just as suddenly as it began, Lovelidge found himself back in his bedroom gazing into the eyes of his very concerned wife.

Lovelidge asserts that this experience has changed his life. He no longer fears death. Because he is now comfortable talking about dying to terminally ill people, he spends much of his spare time volunteering for hospice societies.[16]

Testimonies like these seem to confirm the idea that death is the doorway to a blissful, disembodied existence beyond earthly life. In fact, this is perhaps the most widely held view of death and afterlife in North America today. It has become so commonplace that it regularly finds its way into "pop" culture expressions ranging from films to newspaper comic strips.

The graveside scene in the movie *Steel Magnolias* (1989) offers an illuminating example. Shelby had died in the prime of life, leaving behind her parents, husband, and young son. The funeral and committal service has just ended. Shelby's mother has remained behind at the grave. Almost immediately she is joined by her close circle of female friends, who are at a loss for the right words to say.

In the midst of the small talk that follows, one of the group, Annel, suggests that they ought to be rejoicing. Then to indicate what she sees as the cause for such an absurd idea, she offers the grieving mother her personal theory about what Shelby's death really means. Annel explains that Shelby's body was simply too weak to care for her little boy and for her mother. "So she went on to a place where she could be a guardian angel." In that glorious place beyond death, Annel states confidently, "she will always be young; she will always be beautiful." And, Annel adds, "I personally feel much safer knowing she's up there on my side."

The idea that death marks the transition to a place where the disembodied soul experiences eternal bliss has been highly influential throughout Christian history as well. In an edict of 1336, Pope Benedict XII declared that beginning with death the souls of the righteous enjoy face-to-face contemplation of the divine essence. The souls of the wicked, in contrast, descend to hell (although they will still give an account of their deeds on judgment day).[17]

Despite its wide acceptance and its apparent affinity with the Christian faith, the belief that death is the doorway to eternal bliss is fraught with dangers. Like the idea of reincarnation, it assumes that our true humanness resides in some mysterious nonphysical reality called the "soul." In addition, to see death as the doorway to eternal bliss tempts us to surmise that immortality is somehow something we ourselves possess, rather than being God's gift to us.

But above all, viewing the soul as immortal undercuts the centrality of the resurrection. Why should I look forward to the day when I will rise bodily from the dead, if at death the true "me" floats off to enjoy eternal bliss in some heavenly realm beyond the universe? If death marks the doorway into a glorious spiritual realm, why is Jesus' resurrection so important?

Resurrected Life:
The Source of Hope in the Face of Death

The grand event that shattered the power of death and unleashed a new hope in human hearts occurred on the third day after the Romans crucified a Jewish prophet. On that day, God raised Jesus of Nazareth from the dead. Because of Jesus' resurrection, we can have assurance that Sheol does not speak the last word. On the contrary, this event demonstrated that God is greater than death's power and that God's goal for us is not death but life—eternal life, life in fellowship with God. Through Christ, we can look beyond death to the eternal community God promises us, which we will one day enjoy.

But what marks the doorway into that life? According to the New Testament, the gateway to that eternal reality is not death. Instead, we enter the fullness of life as embodied persons through the resurrection of the dead.

The Hope of Resurrection. The New Testament writers elevate Jesus' resurrection not only as the foundation for our hope beyond death but also as the model for our future overcoming of death. For both Jesus and us, resurrection is marked by continuity and discontinuity—sameness and difference. The risen Lord who appeared to the disciples was the same Jesus they had known prior to his crucifixion. Both his body and his mannerisms bore recognizable resemblances to the Jesus they knew. Yet, Jesus' resurrection was not merely the resuscitation of a corpse. Jesus did not return to earthly life as we now know it. Instead, he had been raised to the life of the age to come.

So also with us. Through resurrection we will enter the fullness of community as the individual persons that we are, for this community will be an eternal fellowship of persons. At the same time, entrance into the fullness of life requires a radical change. This change is physical. Therefore, through the resurrection God will transform our mortality—our susceptibility to disease and death—into immortality. The resurrection change will also be ethical. God will root out our susceptibility to sin and replace it with complete conformity to Christ. In this manner, the resurrection marks God's final no to the workings of death in our lives.

The hope of resurrection offers the only genuine source of comfort to people grieving for friends and relatives whom death has claimed. The good news of a future, glorious day when God will raise the dead means that though we mourn the temporary loss of those we love, as Christians we need not grieve like humans "who have no hope." Instead, we can "encourage one another with these words"—with reminders of God's promise of a future resurrection (1 Thess. 4:13, 18).

The teaching about the resurrection also provides a crucial reminder about who we are as human beings. It confirms that we are by nature physical beings. Because we do not enter the fullness of eternity apart from the body, bodily existence is part of what it means to be human.

In addition, this teaching confirms the communal nature of human life. We do not enter eternity alone, through some individual experience of death. Instead, we begin the fullness of God's destiny for us together. This means that we are not self-sufficient, isolated individuals, but social beings—individuals-in-community.

Hope in the Face of Death. Because we have this hope beyond death, we also have hope in the face of death. The prospect of dying and the thought of our own death need no longer hold terror for us. Death is no longer the isolating, solitary experience it once was. On the contrary, because Jesus has tasted death for us, we are not abandoned in death but are surrounded by God's love (Rom. 8:34–39).

Having lost its ultimacy, death can even carry positive significance. Divested of its sting, the last enemy of humankind now marks the completion of our earthly vocation in service to God (2 Tim. 4:7). For those who are martyred because of their testimony to the Savior, death can even become the way of special sacrifice to the one who himself suffered and died for us (2 Tim. 4:6; Phil. 2:17; Rev. 6:9).

What is death? It need no longer be the angst-producing declaration of the meaninglessness of life. But neither is it the doorway to some higher realm. Because God created us as embodied creatures, death remains a foe. Paul the apostle spoke of it as our "last [i.e., final or ultimate] enemy" (1 Cor. 15:26). Nevertheless, it is a defeated foe.

Death's ultimate defeat lies in the future. It will be fully overcome only on that great future day when together we experience the clothing of our mortal bodies with immortality (1 Cor. 15:54–55). Nevertheless, through Christ we experience a foretaste of resurrection in the present. For this reason, we can say confidently with the apostle John, "We know that we have passed from death to life" (1 John 3:14; cf. John 5:24; 8:51).

But *when* does the resurrection occur? This question leads us to the second part of our overarching query: Where is the world going?

Beyond Armageddon: Where Is the World Going?

In July 1994, twenty-one pieces of a comet slammed into Jupiter, causing bruises on the surface almost as big as Earth. One scientist has concluded that every thousand years, our planet is visited by an asteroid with the diameter of a football field, traveling at twenty miles per second. Were such a heavenly invader to land in one of Earth's oceans today, the tidal wave it would generate could kill a million people. If, however, the asteroid were to measure twelve to twenty-four miles in diameter, as did the projectile that struck the Yucatán some 65 million years ago, it might spell the doom of the world's population.[18]

If the ancient Mayan prediction is true that the climax of the five Great Cycles will bring a tremendous global cataclysm in the near future (specifically, on December 22, 2012), then we may well live to see a natural disaster of catastrophic import.[19]

Despite dire prognostications such as these, many people find the sheer improbability of such a natural disaster a convenient shield from concern. Most, however, are less successful in dismissing the threat of a made-on-earth Armageddon. In fact, we belong to the first generation of humans raised under the specter of nuclear war, the menace of worldwide famine, the shadow of economic chaos, and dire portents of impending ecological disaster—any one of which could destroy the planet.

Not only is Earth vulnerable to a host of potentially devastating forces, both natural and humanly produced, the entire cosmos seems to carry a built-in finitude. Scientists are of divided opinion about what fate lies in the universe's future, but the two most likely scenarios are equally pessimistic. Some anticipate that eventually the force of expansion that arose out of the Big Bang will overcome the counteraction of gravitational attraction and the cosmos will meet its demise in the cold expanse of an eternal cosmic "winter" in which all movement stops. Others speculate that gravity will win out, resulting in the universe being compacted in an apocalyptic Big Crunch.

The fragility of life on Earth as well as the possible demise of the universe itself raises once again Kant's question "What can I hope for?" In the face of the many forces that threaten our planet and our universe, the philosopher's query takes on a cosmic form. Is the human experiment in the end nothing more than the chance result of some unguided—or *mis*guided—process? Is the entire universe merely an interlude between the Big Bang and the Big Crunch? Where is the world going, if anywhere?

The "End" of History

The question "Where are we going?" leads us immediately to the idea of "time" viewed as the connection of events. What joins the isolated incidents that happen in our world?

History or the Circle of Life? In the past, most North Americans assumed that the events on Earth formed a single "story" that includes a starting point in the past and leads eventually to future finish. *History*—understood as the story of humankind—was a common word in our vocabulary. People believed that since its beginning in the distant past, "history" has been moving steadily onward in some sort of inevitable, progressive manner.

The idea of history, however, is by no means the only understanding of time. Its most popular rival claims that rather than forming a linear flow, time is in fact a spiral or perhaps even cyclical. Life, proponents assert, follows a rhythmic pattern—a circle, as it were—of events that occur with observable regularity. This "circle of life" includes such important aspects of existence as the moon's waxing and waning, the changing of the seasons, birth and death. As the theme song of the popular Disney movie *The Lion King* declares, we too "find our place" in the circle of life.

The cyclical view of time boasts a long pedigree that dates back to ancient cultures. In the ancient world, this understanding provided the foundation for a host of religious rituals. The Canaanites living in ancient Palestine, to cite one example, lamented the death of the fertility god Baal and the triumph of Mot the god of death in early summer each year, as the coming drought began to dry out the vegetation. Later, as the winter rains began to replenish the dry ground promising the renewal of vegetation, they celebrated Baal's rebirth.[20]

The Hebrews who settled among the Canaanites and partially dispossessed them came to a different conclusion. Time is not simply cyclical. Nor do events merely follow a repeatable pattern. Instead, each occurrence is ultimately unique. Taken together, events form a trajectory that moves from beginning to end, thereby forming a history. Most importantly, this history is the activity of the one God asserting divine rulership over all the nations of the earth.

In keeping with this understanding, the Hebrew people told a story that began in the distant past in a primeval garden and looked forward to a glorious future. The Old Testament writers bequeathed this historical consciousness to the Christian tradition and through it to Western culture as a whole.

Later, under the impulse of humanism, Western thinkers separated the biblical idea of history from its theological moorage. Moderns no longer thought of linear time as the story of God active in the world, but as the narrative of humankind, or more specifically, of the inevitable advance of human progress. Rather than being "God's story," history became "our story." The goal of this secularized history came to be the construction of a human utopia on earth.

The results of "secular progressivism," as we might call this modern concept of history, were disastrous. Clouds soon began to darken the horizon of the future. The long-anticipated utopia appeared to lie forever out of our reach. Deprived of the sustaining vision of God at work in creation, the secular vision of history could no longer sustain the sense of optimism about the human future. The optimistic ethos gave way to a deep, gnawing pessimism in the hearts of many people, coupled with a growing conviction that the world as we knew it was coming to an end. In the words of Christopher Lasch, "Storm warnings, portents, hints of catastrophe haunt our times. The 'sense of ending,' which has given shape to so much of twentieth century literature, now pervades the popular imagination as well."[21]

Ironically, the current despair about the future is one of the most significant factors contributing to the renewed interest in the cyclical view of time in our society.

History as God's Story. Many people today sense that the world is a dangerous place to live in and that the future is bleak. In this pessimistic context, the Christian message offers hope— not because of what humans are capable of accomplishing, but because God has a purpose for creation. History, viewed as God's story, does have an end—a God-given telos toward which all creation is moving and from which history takes its meaning. Rather than an illusive human utopia that we are ultimately powerless to create, history's goal is nothing less than the glorious realization of God's purposes for creation.

But what exactly is that goal? And how does it arrive? We tackle the second question first.

Jesus' Return in Judgment

What lies at the boundary between our present and God's future? Christians believe that the central event marking the end of history as we know it is the return of the risen and exalted Christ. We can't determine all that this means or exactly how Jesus' return will occur. Nor can we smugly conclude that this promise undercuts the doomsday scenarios prognosticators now forecast.

We do know that Jesus' glorious return will mark our resurrection, which comprises God's final "No!" to death and the inauguration of eternity. But Jesus' return marks the end of history in another manner as well. This event entails God's judgment on that history.

The Judgment of All Creation. The second coming of Jesus marks the judgment of creation. This will include, of course, the cosmic powers. Although Christ has in one sense already judged them on the cross (Col. 2:15), on that future day angels and demons will come under divine scrutiny (Matt. 25:41). And, of course, this will be the devil's day of reckoning, as "our ancient foe" is banished from God's eternal community (Rev. 20:10).

In addition, Jesus' return will entail the judgment of the physical creation (2 Peter 3:10). The goal of this scrutiny is not the destruction of creation but its liberation from the bondage that characterizes its present situation. Here judgment refers to God's act of purging the power of decay and death to prepare the universe for the fellowship God intends to share with all creation. Decay and death must be banished so that creation can be a fitting home for resurrected humankind. But even more significant, one day God will leave the heavenly abode beyond the world and dwell within creation (Rev. 21:1–3). The presence of the eternal God of life requires that the physical realm be cleansed from the power of decay and death. When this happens, the entire cosmos will be free to join together in glorifying the glorious Creator.

Jesus' return will likewise mark the judgment of human beings. Its repeated presence in "pop" culture, evidenced for example in the powerful judgment scenes in both the inaugural and concluding episodes of *Star Trek: The Next Generation,* bears witness to how well ingrained this idea is in people's imaginations. But in contrast to the typical picture of that great day—a vast line of individuals passing by a judge's bench where they receive the final verdict—judgment will occur swiftly, even instantaneously, for it entails the making public of hidden realities (Luke 8:17).

Why must these hidden realities come to light? One reason is to vindicate God. Throughout history, evil—not God—appears to be in control of the world. At Jesus' return, however, God will act decisively to bring about justice in creation (Luke 18:1–8; 2 Peter 3:3–10). When this happens, all will see that God has been neither impotent nor slow to act.

The judgment will mark God's final vindication of Jesus as well, for at the Lord's return all will acknowledge his rulership (Phil. 2:9–11). This event also will confirm that Jesus revealed to us the divine design for humankind, namely, that we live in fellowship with and obedience to God. Our Lord will be the standard in comparison to whom our lives will be measured. The contrast between how we have lived and Jesus' life will result in a gaping disparity, as we see how we focused on the accumulation of earthly possessions to the exclusion of true wealth (Mark 10:17–31; Luke 12:13–21), how we failed to care for the disadvantaged (Matt. 25:31–46), and how we were so slow to forgive (Matt. 18:21–35).

These aspects indicate that the public disclosure of Christ's glory also will reverse human social conditions. At the present time the powerful appear to be in control. On that day, however, all will see that God does not measure success according to earthly understandings of power and prestige but in accordance with Jesus' teachings about humble servanthood and service to others (Matt. 25:31–46; Mark 10:35–45). When this comes to light, the first will indeed be last and the last first.

For this reason, the judgment day will bring surprises. Not all who call Jesus "Lord" will enter the kingdom. To those who offered "lip service" but whose hearts were far away from God, the Judge will respond, "I never knew you" (Matt. 7:21–23). Others will discover that though they are saved, they rendered only meager service to their Lord (1 Cor. 3:15).

The Dark Side of the Judgment. Most people today continue to give at least passing acknowledgment to the reality that the judgment will inaugurate an unhappy fate for some. A poll conducted in 1986 indicated that 67 percent of Americans believe in hell. A similar sampling in 1997 netted a 63 percent positive response.[22] And who will be there? The earlier poll suggested that the respondents anticipated that perhaps as few as 60 percent of their friends are heaven-bound, whereas at least one in four will certainly be in hell.[23]

The reality of hell is a great mystery, but perhaps we can begin to understand its awful reality when we remind ourselves that God is the avenging protector of the love relationship God desires to enjoy with all creation. Those who spurn God's love or seek to destroy this holy relationship experience the divine love as protective jealousy or wrath. Because God is eternal, the experience of God's love in the form of wrath also must be eternal. This is hell.

Hell, however, is not something we announce gleefully. On the contrary, it is "the eternal tragedy," the final, sad outworking of human failure. Lamentably, some creatures whom God loves spurn the divine love, choosing instead not to live in accordance with the purpose of their existence. One day the "shrill dissonance" between their lives and the wonderful destiny God intended for us will be brought to light. Throughout eternity some will suffer gnawing despair as they realize the missed purpose that characterizes their existence and yet remain set in their enmity toward God.

Thanks be to God, however. The divine patience is not yet exhausted. The God who does not delight in the death of the wicked (Ezek. 18:23; 1 Tim. 2:4) continues to offer grace to wayward humans, and the Holy Spirit continues to call them to enter into a fellowship that will continue throughout all eternity.

God's Eternal Community—Our Home

Where is the world going? It is hurtling headlong not toward an eternal Armageddon but to its final goal, conformity with what has been the Creator's purpose from the beginning. What is this purpose? God is bringing about the fulfillment of Jesus' petition: "Your kingdom come. Your will be done, on earth as it is in heaven" (Matt. 6:10). Thereby, our Creator and Savior is preparing an eternal home for us (John 14:1–3).

A New Creation. Throughout the ages people have wondered what might await us in eternity. Typically the word people use to designate the glorious place is *heaven*. What is this realm? A question posed in a 1997 opinion poll reflected the popular characterization: "Do you believe in the existence of heaven, where people live forever with God after they die?" An astounding 81 percent of those queried offered a positive response to the question.[24] As this wording of the survey query suggests, many people conceive of heaven as an entirely "spiritual" (nonmaterial) realm inhabited by purely spiritual beings.

Despite the widespread belief that our eternal home is a realm beyond the world, "the new creation" is a more helpful designation. Our final abode is not completely disconnected from the universe we now inhabit. Instead, it is in some sense a physical realm—not simply the universe as it now is but the cosmos purified and transformed, and thereby brought into conformity with the divine design. This is what the biblical seers meant when they spoke about God making "all things new" and creating "a new heaven and a new earth" (Isa. 65:17; Rev. 21:1). Not only will the renewed earth be our eternal home, but God also will take up residence there with us (Rev. 21:3). The eternal God plans to dwell with reconciled humans in the new creation!

The new creation will differ greatly from the reality we now experience. God will banish from our eternal home everything that is harmful or stands counter to the Creator's perfect design. Above all, God will expunge every trace of the evil alien power that now endeavors to keep us in bondage. God will likewise eradicate decay, disease, and most importantly death (Rom. 8:21; Rev. 21:4). Gone will be the sense of uncertainty, insecurity, anxiety, and despair (Heb. 11:10; 12:28). No one will ever again undergo suffering or go wanting for the necessities that sustain life (Rev. 22:1–3a).

Although in this manner the old will give way to the new, God does not intend to replace the cosmos in its physicality with some purely nonmaterial, "heavenly" realm. On the contrary, it is *this* universe that God will transform into the new creation, thereby bringing about God's original intent for creation.

A Community. What will our new home be like? In a word: "community," or better still—the "fullness of community." Community will characterize our home because the triune God is present. John the seer reported, "And I heard a loud voice from the throne saying, 'See the home of God is among mortals. He will dwell with them'" (Rev. 21:3). At the end of history, the transcendent Creator of the universe willingly and graciously chooses to leave the lofty realm beyond the world to become fully immanent in creation.

For this reason, we will enjoy complete fellowship with the triune God. Now we sense a great gulf separating us from our Maker: God is in heaven and we are on the earth (Eccl. 5:2). Then, however, we will see our Lord "as he is" (1 John 3:2) and bathe in the radiance of the divine presence. As resurrected people, we will also enjoy fellowship with one another, and because the old curse due to our human failure is lifted, we will be at peace with all creation (Rev. 22:2–3).

The new community will be not only a glorious realm but also a place of glorification. We will join together with all creation in glorifying God as the Spirit molds us into one great chorus of praise to the eternal Father after the pattern of Jesus the Son (John 17:4). As we offer our praise and service to God, we find ourselves fulfilling the very goal of our existence, and the Father in turn glorifies us, just as he eternally loves the Son (John 17:24).

Hope for the Future
and Hope in the Present

Although its fullness lies in the future, God has already inaugurated the eternal community awaiting us in the new heaven and new earth. Despite the brokenness of the present, through Christ and because of the presence of the Holy Spirit, we can already enjoy a foretaste of the complete fellowship that will one day be ours.

Rather than longing to escape from the world, the glorious hope that we will one day enjoy fullness of fellowship in God's new community ought to motivate us to diligent engagement in the world. It should lead us to redouble our efforts in service to others for Christ's sake. At the conclusion of his extended discussion of our future resurrection, Paul offers this forceful admonition: "Therefore, my beloved, be steadfast, immovable, always excelling in the work of the Lord, because you know that in the Lord your labor is not in vain" (1 Cor. 15:56).

NOTES

1. "Mass Suicide Suspected as 39 Men Found Dead in California Mansion," *The Vancouver Sun* (March 27, 1997): A1; "Emergence of Grim Details Underlines Cult Tragedy," *The Vancouver Sun* (March 29, 1997): A9.
2. Marci McDonald, "Towards the Year 2000," *Maclean's* 108, no. 52 (Dec. 25, 1995–Jan. 1, 1996): 29. See also p. 20.
3. Immanuel Kant, *Critique of Pure Reason*, trans. Norman Kemp Smith (London: Macmillan, 1933), A805/B833, p. 635.
4. Saul Bellow, *Herzog* (New York: Viking, 1964), 289–90.
5. "U.S. Preteens Living with Fear, Poll Says," *The Vancouver Sun* (May 12, 1995): A19.
6. Mary Nemeth, "An Alarming Trend," *Maclean's* 107, no. 44 (Oct. 31, 1994): 15.
7. Gerry Bellett, "We Have Lived Our Lives and This Life Is Not for Us—Goodbye," *The Vancouver Sun* (October 20, 1994): B4.
8. "A Matter of Responsibility," *Maclean's* 107, no. 32 (Aug. 8, 1994): 36.
9. George Eldon Ladd, *The Last Things* (Grand Rapids: Eerdmans, 1978), 32.
10. James Redfield, *The Celestine Prophecy: An Adventure* (New York: Warner Books, 1993), 242–43.
11. Rosemary Radford Ruether, *Sexism and God-Talk* (Boston: Beacon, 1983), 258.
12. Barbara Wickens, "I Was Guinevere," *Maclean's* 109, no. 9 (Feb. 26, 1996): 71.
13. See Plato's dialogue *Phaedo*, 70c-d, where reincarnation is referred to as an "ancient tradition." See also *Phaedo* 70–77, 80d; *The Republic* 609–21; *Timacus* 41d–42d; *Meno* 81–86b.

14. Plato, *Phaedo* 64a–69e, in *The Collected Dialogues of Plato*, ed. Edith Hamilton and Huntington Cairns (Princeton: Princeton University Press, 1961), 46–52.
15. This term has been in vogue since the appearance of Raymond A. Moody, Jr., *Life after Life* (Covington, Ga.: Mockingbird Books, 1975).
16. Jamie Baxter, "Death: The Experience of a Lifetime," *The Vancouver Sun* (July 29, 1995): C10.
17. *Constitutio Benedictina*, in *The Church Teaches: Documents of the Church in English Tradition*, trans. John F. Clarkson et al. (St. Louis: Herder, 1955), 349–51.
18. Tim Radford, "Why Actuaries Worry about Asteroids," *The Vancouver Sun* (November 4, 1995): B2.
19. See John Oliphant, "A People of Vision," *The Vancouver Sun* (February 17, 1996): D11.
20. Hans-Joachim Kraus, *Worship in Israel: A Cultic History of the Old Testament*, trans. G. Bushwell (Richmond, Va.: John Knox, 1966), 38–43.
21. Christopher Lasch, *The Culture of Narcissism: American Life in an Age of Diminishing Expectations* (New York: Norton, 1978), 3.
22. David Van Biema, "Does Heaven Exist?" *Time* 149, no. 12 (March 24, 1997): 73.
23. "Poll: Most People Think They're Heaven-Bound," Sioux Falls *Argus Leader* (December 16, 1986): 3A.
24. Van Biema, "Does Heaven Exist?" 73.